DATE

Those Europeans

Studies of Foreign Faces

Those Europeans

Studies of Foreign Faces

By

Sisley Huddleston

Essay Index Reprint Series

BOOKS FOR LIBRARIES PRESS
FREEPORT, NEW YORK

First Published 1924
Reprinted 1969

STANDARD BOOK NUMBER:
8369-1218-7

LIBRARY OF CONGRESS CATALOG CARD NUMBER:
79-90647

PRINTED IN THE UNITED STATES OF AMERICA

CONTENTS

iii

iv   Contents

Those Europeans:
Studies of Foreign Faces

Those Europeans: Studies of Foreign Faces

I

MACDONALD: THE SYMBOL OF ENGLAND'S STRENGTH

RAMSAY MACDONALD is a portent. He is a portent of new things to come. He is a symbol. He is a symbol of the strength of England.

England has remained throughout the changing centuries supreme and unassailable because always at need could she produce new men with new ideas; new men who did not seek to apply their new ideas in revolutionary fashion, who did not dream of breaking the continuity of things, who were in the true line of tradition, but who, nevertheless, rejuvenated tradition, and infused new blood into custom.

Whenever England is menaced, whenever

things go awry, whenever the governing classes, as they are called, grow weary and effete, England reaches down, as it were, to her roots and she produces a new type of man, a man capable of renovations, a man who, however alien he may be to the governing classes, is accepted by them because they realise that he is necessary.

The conception of Hilaire Belloc—which in some measure corresponds to the truth—is that of a close corporation, an inner ring of politicians who, generation after generation, carry on in England. They are recruited from the ruling families. It is not merely the House of Lords to which applies the hereditary principle. The House of Commons and the Governments are also institutions based upon the hereditary principle. But breaking into this charmed circle, there arises from time to time a man who can more fittingly represent the spirit of the age, who has precisely the qualities which are needed at a particular moment, and which the ruling families cannot themselves supply. According to this theory, although the personnel of the inner ring may change, it changes by co-option from inside rather than by imposition from outside.

Many cases could be cited in which for generations father has succeeded son in governmental affairs, either in the deliberative assembly or in the administration—now a Minister, then an Ambassador, and then again perhaps the permanent head of a government department. Cases could be cited in which members of the same family place themselves, it would seem deliberately, on opposite sides of the House—one on the Liberals, the other on the Conservative side—so that whatever may be the forces which make for an alternation of power, one member of the family at least shall have some share of authority.

All this is, of course, far too diagrammatic: it is an exaggeration; but it nevertheless forms, as it were, the background of the English system. It is to be observed, however, that most of the notable figures in British parliamentary history in the long line of Prime Ministers, from the first Pitt to Ramsay Macdonald, have been co-opted from outside. A Balfour might follow in the footsteps of a Salisbury, but the Gladstones, Disraelis, Lloyd Georges, Chamberlains (in each case I am speaking of the original bearer of that name in parliamentary life) are thrust into the system and have renovated and justified the system.

Lloyd George, when he first emerged, was a new phenomenon, but he was a healthy phenomenon. He represented the revolt against the selfish insolence of vested interests; he helped perhaps to stave off a more violent reaction against the greed of those who ground the faces of the poor. He rendered his country signal service. He was young, ardent, alert, until in the end success spoilt him and he became fat, comfortable, and lazy, without the snap and the instinct of former days. England had found, unconsciously as it were, the man who was needed.

But nothing could represent this truth more forcibly than the advent of Ramsay Macdonald, the first Labour Prime Minister of England. For Ramsay Macdonald came to power without even a parliamentary majority. He was a Prime Minister on sufferance. Why, when Socialism was abhorred by Liberals and Conservatives alike, was he permitted to take office with a minority of votes? Why was he permitted to continue in power for months when at any moment the Liberals and Conservatives voting together might upset him? Nor would it be true to suggest that during the early months of his stay in office he avoided controversial subjects. Sometimes the Conservatives would be incensed against him and would endeavour to overthrow him in their anger. But the Liberals would save him. Sometimes the Liberals would arise in their wrath to destroy Ramsay Macdonald and his somewhat incompetent Cabinet, but then the Conservatives rushed to his rescue.

The secret is plain enough. England knew that she needed a new man. She had suffered sufficiently from the older statesmen and she was not willing to return to the simple method of putting in a formerly discredited Liberal and putting out a discredited Conservative, who in turn would come a few years later to replace the again discredited Liberal.

Asquith had made a mess of the war: Lloyd George had made a mess of the peace: Bonar Law and Baldwin and Curzon had made between them the most frightful mess of British foreign policy. Should the country, then, return to Asquith or Lloyd George? All parties were conscious that something more than the con-

tinuance of the game of ins and outs was needed.
It was a critical moment for England, who had
lost her prestige on the Continent of Europe,
and while stupidly making concession after concession in an effort to obtain American friendship
had merely succeeded in arousing American
suspicion. When the Greeks bring gifts . . .

Toryism in England had become effete. It
had fallen into the hands of business men who
understood nothing of government and of diplomacy, and into the hands of aristocrats, who
understood rather too much about government
and diplomacy, but made the mistake of assuming that England was peopled by Hindus, and
that the Continent was merely another India, to
which consular persons could haughtily dictate
their wishes. Lord Curzon had indulged in his
superior art of writing crushing Notes, and of
even forbidding M. Poincaré to deliver a friendly
message by wireless telephony on New Year's
Day to the British people, until Franco-British
relations had become as embittered as they well
could be.

The Liberal Party, though with a great
historical past, was not yet reconstructed after
its rending asunder by the war. It was time that

somebody new, with a new party, were found, to save England from the mistakes of the obsolete men and the obsolete parties.

It was the porridge-eating, simple living, cautious but clearsighted Scotsman, Ramsay Macdonald, who was clearly, as the doctors say, "indicated." To illustrate the change, I may repeat a story which is perhaps apocryphal but which ought to be true. The first day that a high dignitary from the Foreign Office brought his report to Ramsay Macdonald, the successor of Lord Curzon, the Prime Minister, who was also acting as his own Foreign Secretary, waved him to a seat. The high dignitary ignored the gesture. "But why don't you sit down?" asked Ramsay Macdonald. The official pretended not to hear; but Macdonald insisted. "Surely, you will be more comfortable, and we can discuss this matter better, if you take a chair." "Do you really mean," said the official, "that in your presence I should sit down?" Let us assume that this story is a malicious invention, if you please, but it does serve to show the difference of spirit of the two governments. The Macdonald government, like Macdonald himself, was homely, familiar and polite, in the

true sense of the word. It was anxious about
results and not about appearances. It got down
to business and refused to stand on its dignity.

Even M. Poincaré was treated as a fellow
human being. This was of the utmost importance, for you cannot be supercilious to the
French if you wish to obtain anything from
them. Circumstances might be too much for
both Ramsay Macdonald and for Poincaré,
but at least there would be a better chance of
agreement between France and England—and
without agreement nothing whatever could be
accomplished, except the destruction of Europe
—if the two countries could only recover some of
the old friendly spirit. Nothing is too elementary to say nowadays, and I therefore make no
apology for declaring sententiously that two
nations who have good feeling towards each other
are much more likely to discover a common
policy than two nations who are quarrelling
with each other.

It may not appear to be a signal proof of
Ramsay Macdonald's ability and insight that
he should have rediscovered this exceedingly
simple truth, but it was undoubtedly a great
service that he rendered to Europe in suddenly

reminding it that soft words turn away wrath; that if you wish to come to terms, it is advisable to begin by creating an atmosphere in which it is possible to talk reasonably.

Nothing will help us, perhaps, to understand better the character of Ramsay Macdonald than his return to the rudiments of diplomacy. One of the faults of our age is that it is too clever by half. Macdonald was brought up in what was called in England a Board School. He had not the disadvantage of a training at the Universities of Oxford and of Cambridge. Happily, he never went to Eton or to Harrow. Board schools—I believe they are now known as Council Schools—endeavour to give an elementary education, and an elementary education given by teachers who themselves spring from the people, coupled with a personal experience of the hardships and realities of life, is infinitely better than what is alleged to be the higher education in unrealities.

Macdonald could hardly go wrong, assuming that he were a man gifted with common sense. He knew; he had a proper humility; he did not suppose himself to be superior to the facts of experience. He applied to the art of government and of diplomacy the same principles that he learnt in the Board School.

What I like, too, about him is that he does not endeavour to camouflage his obscure origins or his elementary education. It is written large in the English *Who's Who* for all who care to read it. He does not leave out the Board School. He puts it in challengingly, proudly. This explains much.

Macdonald was never a rich man, remote from the real world. He had to rise by sheer force of will, by keeping a constant grip on things, by remaining in contact with the people. But this does not mean that he is without culture. It does not mean that he is without knowledge. On the contrary, such a man has a far better chance of acquiring practical knowledge and true culture than those who have all kinds of artificial advantages.

Moreover, he was aided enormously by his wife, Margaret Ethel Gladstone, the daughter of a distinguished professor. When she died in 1911, he paid the most moving tribute to her memory. The little Scottish lad, who, like many of his race, strove in adverse circumstances to furnish his mind, undoubtedly owes much to the graceful, kindly creature who was his companion for many years.

Her death marked the beginning of a series of misfortunes. In the Labour Party he had for some years made great headway. From 1900 to 1911 he had acted as Secretary of the Party, and for three years—from 1906 to 1909—he had been Chairman of the Independent Labour Party. He was recognised as the parliamentary leader until 1914, but he then seemed to be a broken man. When the war came he found himself unable to indulge in the demagogy that most of the politicians in England thought fit to indulge in. He fell into disgrace, into complete unpopularity. There were other Labour leaders who became the most voracious fire-eaters. They out-Heroded Herod. Some of them even entered the War Government. Macdonald remained aloof, saddened, crushed. He almost lost faith. It is, I think, betraying no secret to say that to those who could understand, to whom he could unbosom his soul, he questioned, during the dreadful years of war and during the still more dreadful years of peacemaking—for during the war one was, at any rate, sustained by noble, unselfish passions, but during the years

of peacemaking, selfishness and ignoble passions
ran riot—whether it was worth while going on.

All for which he had striven seemed to be in
ruins around him. His hopes were wrecked:
the cause for which he had fought all his life, the
cause of the oppressed and the cause of international fraternity, seemed to have received
a definite and permanent set-back. He was
disheartened. One scurrilous publicist and
swindler, who loudly boasted of his patriotism,
and whom an ungrateful country has since put
in gaol for a long term of years for defrauding the
poor, persistently endeavoured to hound him
out of public life, not so much on the ground of
his opinions as on the ground of his humble
birth. He nearly succeeded. But in the end
the wheel of fortune turned; the patriot was in
prison, the despised and rejected of men was—
even without a parliamentary majority—made
Prime Minister of England.

There were many others in his own party who
had, it would appear, prior claims to the Leadership. Macdonald had been out of parliamentary life for some years. He came back only in
1922. He had, however, improved his time
in travel, so that he is certainly one of the most

travelled men in England, knowing at first hand
many foreign countries.

I met him in those days on his way through
France, where he kept in close touch with the
French Socialist Leaders. He was still a handsome man, with his grey hair, his deeply wrinkled
forehead, his quiet, thoughtful eyes, and the
strong features of his face. He was always
unassuming, always simple. He. did not speak
over much, preferring to listen and to puff
meditatively his pipe. But he was learning all
the time, and he made use of his knowledge to
earn a modest living as a journalist. He was
not, in my opinion, a first-rate journalist. His
style is not particularly distinguished, but it
was like the man, conscientious, clear, exact,
cautious.

His family life—Macdonald has three sons
and two daughters—was happy. Without much
means, he managed to provide a good education
for his children and to bring them up as useful
citizens. His passage at Downing Street and at
Chequers, among sumptuous surroundings, to
which he had not been accustomed, will leave
him and his children as unaffected as ever. He
is of that stalwart Scottish blood, that is not

marred by fortune. When he goes out, he will return to his modest Hampstead home.

Some misguided persons in England began an agitation to provide ex-Prime Ministers with a large pension. They considered that it was a reflection on the country that a former Prime Minister should ever return to the simple life. They considered that for the future he should be in a position to uphold the dignity of the country. Their idea of dignity is to possess riches. Macdonald scornfully refused the proffered gift. Could he not always earn sufficient for his wants, which were few? Could he not be equally dignified in working for the newspapers, in saying what there was in him to say? Could he not be equally happy as a poor man?

In what does happiness consist? It is not to be bought with gold. A quiet walk on Hampstead Heath, an occasional game of golf, are inexpensive pleasures. Books, too, are inexpensive. Work, also, work in the cause of humanity is inexpensive. It is there that happiness lies, and in the consciousness that one has done one's best to bring up one's family and to leave the world a little better than one found it.

England is well served by her children. She

has been well served at different times by her rich men; by her aristocratic families. But she is no less well served by her common citizens, by the serious-minded and simple representatives of the people, the good little people.

It is the turn of the little people to stand in the front rank and to undo the mischief that has been caused in Europe by those whose rôle is, for the moment at least, ended. Ramsay Macdonald is a portent: Ramsay Macdonald is a symbol.

II

CLEMENCEAU: EUROPE'S GREATEST MAN

OF all the European statesmen that I have known, Georges Clemenceau impresses me as undoubtedly the greatest. I do not say this because—to use the journalistic jargon of the time—Clemenceau is the man who won the war. The greatness of men is to be judged, not by what they do—that is largely accidental, a question of opportunity—but by what they are; and Clemenceau is really wonderful. He is a well of apparently inexhaustible life. He is full of high spirits and has learned how to accept the smiles and frowns of fortune with equal good grace. His talk is that of a man who has thought intensely and who has no longer need to pause for reflection. One feels that he knows everything, has anticipated every incident, is aware of every combination, and like a master chessplayer, realises at a glance the fitting word to say, the fitting deed to do.

Clemenceau is full of the most detestable faults, but one certainly could not detest him. When he was in power he was arbitrary and tyrannical. Some of the men around him were unscrupulous and he himself had no pity for his enemies. He was headstrong and authoritative. The Treaty of Versailles is not a monument which will handsomely perpetuate his memory. There have been dark episodes in his life, some of them undeserved and others which he himself provoked. He has had such ups and downs as few statesmen have had, sometimes reaching the very highest pinnacle of fame, sometimes falling into the lowest pit of utter disgrace. Sometimes the whole nation has clamoured around the pedestal upon which it had placed him, sometimes the whole nation has hissed him out of politics for years. But in good and evil days, M. Clemenceau has shrugged his shoulders, has kept a cheerful countenance, has fortified himself with philosophical contempt for the changeable mob, has turned to his multiple occupations and has bided his time.

The greatness which I have unhesitatingly attributed to him resides in his indomitable character. Character in the English sense of the word is something which no dictionary can define. M. Clemenceau has it. It is better than mere brains, it is independent of physique, it is not courage, it is not even mere rectitude. The bad man, as well as the good man, may have what we call character. The rather dull man, as well as the brilliantly clever man, may have character. But good or bad, dull or clever, it is character that becomes the principal virtue, the dominating feature. There is much to be said of M. Clemenceau's other qualities, but the chief and first thing to say of him is that he possesses this remarkable something to which we give the name of character.

As I have pointed out in one of my books, Clemenceau wears a *panache* of the largest possible kind. Everything he does is somehow spectacular. He has the dramatic imagination which unconsciously works and which gives him the right word and inspires the right gesture at the right moment. Here again, I would like to say that the absence or presence of a panache has absolutely nothing to do with character. There are many quiet, unassuming, undramatic men who have character, too. But one is bound to note especially of M. Clemenceau that whatever he does, he does interestingly; he does it differently; he does it as though he were play-acting, although in fact he is perfectly sincere and in deadly earnest. Even when he is in the deadliest earnestness, however, cheerfulness will keep breaking in. Superficially, he is by no means a serious person. Over everything there plays the lambent flame of his somewhat cynical wit. It is a mistake to suppose that it is wrong to joke about the gravest things. It is precisely the gravest things that are best worth joking about, and the best jokes are those which are made in the most critical circumstances.

It is these men who give a whimsical turn to the most dangerous events, whose malicious spirits make laughter chase out fear, that are the salt of the earth. They help the world to pre-serve its sanity; they make us appreciate men and things in their right perspective. There is a sort of cynicism which exalts, inasmuch as it enables us to see through the whole pretensions of humanity and enables us, even while we are striving desperately for some aim, to understand that all will not be lost, indeed, very little will be lost, even should we fail.

That Clemenceau meant with an iron resolve

that France should win the war, nobody can doubt; but this did not prevent him from seeing and revealing the gayer side of the struggle. He enabled France to endure just because he ridiculed as well as praised, just because he relieved the unbearable tension from time to time by an incongruous reflection.

Clemenceau is exceedingly simple in his tastes. While men around him have grown rich, he has remained poor and despising riches. When he is in his little home in Vendée, he lives on as little as twenty francs a day. It is a tiny one-storey building, such as would please a peasant. In Paris, Clemenceau lives in a *bourgeois* house which is let out in flats. The last time I visited him there, the *concierge* was cleaning the court by flinging a pail of water upon it. There was no smartness, no flunkeyism. Behind the flat of M. Clemenceau at the bottom of the court, there is a diminutive garden; trees tap against the window-panes. The furniture is old and somewhat shabby. But although I said just now that M. Clemenceau is relatively poor, he possesses artistic treasures galore—pictures by Claude Monet, statuary by Rodin—the works of most of the great artists of his time, with whom

he was particularly friendly. For it is a mistake
to suppose that M. Clemenceau is a politician
and nothing but a politician.

He was the companion of Alphonse Daudet,
Edmond de Goncourt, Cézanne, whose cause he
was among the first to champion, and Octave
Mirbeau. Some of his art criticisms are among
the finest appreciations that have been written
during the past half century. There is notably
his wonderful article on the series of paintings
by Claude Monet: *Les Cathedrales de Rouen.*
He encouraged the sculptor, Constantin Meunier.
He paid fine tribute to de Goncourt. But, indeed, Clemenceau is one of those rare men who
have touched life at almost every point. Usually
your politician is a narrow person who knows
nothing besides his *métier.* But while the politician is often the narrowest of men, the journalist,
that is to say, the best journalist, is generally
the broadest of men. Clemenceau was essentially the journalist who was interested in every
manifestation of life, who flung himself with zest
into everything that was happening around him.

If he wrote against the government and
became the terrible tumbler of Ministries, he was
at the same time fighting with Edouard Manet,

who had scandalised the public with his modernist paintings, against the Philistines. He ranged himself, too, on the side of Zola in the defence of Dreyfus. He was the greatest polemist of his day. If one considers the energy with which he flung himself into the battle about Dreyfus alone, he has ample claims to be long remembered. Day after day he wrote the most inspiring articles. They have been collected into seven big volumes and although they naturally deal with day by day developments, one is still stirred to indignation in reading them. They quiver with passion, but every now and again the inexpugnable irony of Clemenceau asserts itself, and it may be that his mirth, bitter as it was, did more for the cause than his denunciation.

Clemenceau was courageous, indefatigable, on the whole on the side of truth and of justice. Sometimes it was at the risk of their lives that Zola and Clemenceau left the Palais de Justice.

But, indeed, any consideration of his life will show that he was not content with a mere armchair existence as writer, or with a mere oratorical display as politician. He has lived his life to the full; he has experienced everything.

Once I was told that the only complete character in history or fiction is Ulysses, who was husband, father, lover, statesman, warrior, wanderer, poet—whose life was as comprehensive as life can well be. When one goes through the great names of history and fiction, it will be seen that there is much truth in the contention that the all-round great man can hardly be found. One man may be a philosopher but be inactive. Another may be a warrior but may not have expressed himself in words. Another may be a statesman but may never have seen the world.

Now, Clemenceau has been everything. Let us résumé briefly his story. As a youth he was thrown into the royal prison for his violent speeches. He became mayor of Montmartre, and stayed in his post throughout the dreadful days of the French defeat by Germany. As a young man he went to America, wrote for a French newspaper, learnt English and became a professor in a school at Greenwich, Connecticut. It was there that he met with the young pupil whom he afterwards married.

On his return to France he had seventeen years of parliamentary and of journalistic life. They were years of incessant action. He was involved in the movement of General Boulanger and in the notorious Panama affair. It was a cartoon in the *Petit Journal* depicting him to be juggling with bags of British gold that finally drove him out of public life. Ernest Judet was then the editor of the *Petit Journal* and Clemenceau never forgave him. Many years later, during the great war, Judet was accused of commerce with the enemy but was in the end acquitted.

When Clemenceau had fallen into public disgrace, he simply turned his attention to other occupations. He became the man of letters. *La Mêlée Sociale, Les Plus Forts, Le Grand Pan, Le Voile du Bonheur* are some of his works, which are certainly alive and intense. He threw himself into every movement of his time. He was sixty years of age when he was elected to the Senate and began a new parliamentary career. Late in life he become Minister in the Sarrien Cabinet, in which also figured Bourgeois, Poincaré, Briand, Leguyes, Barthou, Doumergue. As Minister of the Interior, Clemenceau suppressed the strikes in the North with characteristic vigour, but he did not fear to go among the inflamed strikers and to address them—a piece of *cranerie* which was typical of Clemenceau, and which impressed even the most turbulent strikers.

It is curious that when a little later he was himself asked to head a new Government, among his Ministers were Viviani and Joseph Caillaux. Once more he displayed extraordinary energy during the winegrowers' revolt of 1907. Something like civil war was feared in the four Départements of Languedoc. Bridges were burnt or blown up on the Canal du Midi. Soldiers mutinied, barricades were erected at Narbonne; but Clemenceau was at once ruthless and a peacemaker.

Clemenceau foresaw the war. His public life may be said to have begun with the defeat of France by Germany, and to have ended with the defeat of Germany by France and her allies. Clemenceau was one of the makers of the Entente Cordiale with England. He met King Edward at Marienbad after the interviews that the British King had with the German and Austrian Emperors.

There is no doubt that Clemenceau lived with the hope of seeing the tables turned on Germany, and if he did not use the victory which came to France altogether wisely, it should be remembered that the humiliation of 1870 had sunk very deeply into the minds of patriotic Frenchmen.

When Caillaux surrendered a portion of the Congo in return for a freer hand in Morocco and also—for this is the key to the situation— to prevent Germany from making war again on France, Clemenceau launched a formidable attack on his former collaborator. Caillaux was replaced at the beginning of 1912 by Raymond Poincaré, who, after a year of office, became President of the French Republic. France had determined to stand up to Germany, and it was only a question of when the war would begin. It cannot be said that although Clemenceau's popularity grew during the first three years of the war, that he was entirely helpful. He could not forget that he had become above all a fiery polemist. He attacked the successive governments and took his part in upsetting them. Although he advocated the institution of a censorship, he was bound to become one of its first victims. His own newspaper, *L'Homme Libre*, was suppressed and he promptly changed the title to *L'Homme Enchaîné*.

But when he was called to power in 1917, he did splendid work in checking *défaiteism*, in

stimulating the French people, who were weary of
the war, and in inspiring the French soldiers, who
were beginning openly to mutiny. Spies and
traitors, and some who were not spies or traitors,
were arrested wholesale. Caillaux was one of
the persons arrested. Foch was made general-
issimo. The American troops began to pour in.
Clemenceau was omnipotent and omnipresent,
flashing from point to point; one day at the
Tribune, making such discourses as that which
has for refrain, "Je fais la guerre"; the next in
the front line trenches, cheering the soldiers
with his rough jocularity.

No man approaching eighty years of age has
ever been so active as he was; and had he
resigned office when the war ended, when he had
reached his apotheosis, it would perhaps have
been well. Unfortunately, he continued in
power and is one of the authors of the Versailles
Treaty which was drawn up by men who could
not help, in spite of the principles of President
Wilson, being vindictive and unpractical after
the great war, men who could not look ahead,
who could not understand that victories cannot
be stereotyped, that the Allies cannot remain for
ever in an attitude of triumph with their foot on

the neck of Germany. He sat there in the councils of statesmen, his grey-gloved hands outspread, opposing every concession.

The French people did not know why and where he had erred. They thought he had erred in being too lenient, when, in fact, he had erred in not ending the war by a real treaty of peace. But they knew he had erred, and when he presented himself as candidate for the Presidency in 1920, they suddenly threw down their idol and blamed him for all the misfortunes of peace, all the disappointments, all the disasters.

"I wanted to be President," he told me afterwards, "although I realise that I have suddenly become an old man. I wanted to be President, not for long, but to crown my career." But Clemenceau had become accustomed to ingratitude during his long life, and he did not complain.

M. Clemenceau after his lapse into silence— broken only by his triumphant tour through the United States—let it be known that his political life had ended. Why should he begin again for an ungrateful people at the age of eighty? He told me, with what truth I do not know, that he contemplated writing a book, the title of which would be, "If I were God."

He works at a great horseshoe table, a yellow desk piled with books and papers and photographs, completely surrounding an island of human energy. It is in this study that he receives his visitors with whom he usually laughs with the hearty laughter of a man in his prime. His conversation is throughout broken by great unaffected guffaws. A man who can laugh—that is an excellent thing. Whether one is prejudiced for or against M. Clemenceau, one has to regard the fact that he laughs constantly and joyously. That is perhaps the secret of his green old age. He makes fun even of his own physical infirmities.

His observations on contemporary French politicians are refreshingly vigorous. They reveal a piercing wit, a keen eye for the weaknesses of his successors, an ability to sum up his impressions in the most scathing and illuminating phrases. But although it stings, there is nothing malicious in his criticism. Here is a man who has lived long, who has learnt how to weigh his colleagues in the balance, who has terrible insight into human nature and who makes merry over the strange comedy.

It is curious that he should despise politics

and politicians as he does, and yet it is not curious since he has in fact never been a politician himself. He has never sought office, he has never tried to ingratiate himself; he has never practised those tactics of the lobby which the politician is obliged to practise, and he has never hesitated to attack anybody. His tongue has lashed his friends as much as his foes.

When asked why he had chosen M. Klotz as Finance Minister, he replied, "Because he is the only Jew who does not understand finance." When asked for whom he would vote at the Presidential election at Versailles which put into opposition M. Poincaré and M. Pams, he said, "My vote goes to the more stupid of the two." When Mr. Wilson put forward his fourteen points, he remarked, "But God was content with ten." There is no end to the stories that could be told of him, but it is sufficient to note that no man who constantly says the most scathing things can be an office seeker. If he was wanted, he was there; and if he did accept power, he exercised it regardless of the consequences. He has always been the *enfant terrible*, doing whatever he desired.

He would have made a wonderful Mongolian

King—he has the Mongolian appearance. The
place of Clemenceau is marked out in history.
He may be regarded as supremely bad or
supremely good; he may be regarded as the evil
genius of the peace or as the incarnation of
patriotism in the war.

No one who has known him, no one who has
felt the enormous vitality of the man, who has
realised that he is a force of nature, can doubt
that for better or for worse, indeed, irrespective
of what he has done or has left undone, irrespective of the circumstances which created the
river bed of his torrential life, M. Clemenceau
is in himself perhaps the greatest man that
Europe has produced in our generation.

III

PROFESSOR THOMAS G. MASARYK is the President of the new little country of Czecho-Slovakia. A few years ago, would-be wits would loudly mouth such names as Czecho-Slovakia and Yugo-Slavia with appropriate facetious remarks. It was considered that the names were quaint and strange, and, therefore, comic. But there is, in fact, nothing of a comic-opera state about Czecho-Slovakia, unless perhaps we concede to the wits its name. It might have been better to have called it Bohemia, but then Bohemia also, though simpler, has its non-serious connotations for facetious persons.

The Republic of Czecho-Slovakia could not have been otherwise named, because it is composed not only of Czechs but of Slovaks, neither of whom would yield to the other. In truth, the

population of this "succession state" is mixed.
Out of thirteen million souls, there are about
three million Germans. There are perhaps a
quarter of a million Magyars, and, be it remembered, that the Czechs are even more bitterly
opposed to Hungary, from which come the
Magyars, than they are to Germany. There
are besides probably half a million Ruthenians.
The Slovaks may number from two and a half
to three millions. The rest of the population is
Czech. These figures are important, for they
indicate at once that even were Czecho-Slovakia
an old well-founded country it would not be
altogether easy to govern a mixed population
of this kind, a population whose sentiments and
ideas differ considerably. But when it is recalled that a few years ago Czecho-Slovakia did
not exist, that it had to be invented, and that
the inventive powers of the members of the
Peace Conference, though exercised freely, were
not of the highest quality, it will be seen that the
task of the first President of this heterogeneous
nation was indeed a difficult one.

No wonder, therefore, that gloomy prophets
have gone about the world proclaiming the
instability of Czecho-Slovakia. How could such

an artificial grouping of peoples be viable?
Theoretically, the gloomy prophets were doubtless right, but they overlooked the genius of
President Masaryk and his exceedingly able
lieutenant, Dr. Edouard Benes.

The facts have given a serious rebuke to the
gloomy prophets. Of all the countries in Central Europe which were created or reconstituted
by the Peace Treaties of 1919,Czecho-Slovakia
has undoubtedly made the greatest progress.
It has settled down; it has consolidated itself;
it has developed its industries; it has inaugurated
what is on the whole a sound foreign policy.
Starting in the worst possible conditions, it has
made good; it has demonstrated its right to
separate existence. After all, the proof of the
pudding is in the eating, and whether one
approves of the theories which guided the peacemakers in the breaking-up of Austro-Hungary,
or whether one deplores them, there can be no
question that Mr. Masaryk and Mr. Benes
have done their work exceedingly well.

Now this means that a remarkable man was
placed at the head of a new state. I have no
hesitation in declaring that Mr. Masaryk is one
of the ablest men in Europe. He has, naturally,

made mistakes, and I have myself criticised very severely some of the errors of the new republic. But on the whole no one could have done better. The former professor was not at first sight the most suitable leader. His appearance is grave and dignified; his manner is reserved and even cold. He belongs to the study and not to the forum, and he is, in short, the professor.

How, then, has this grey-bearded, serious-minded university don, succeeded in constructing a new country in Central Europe? The reasons are manifold. First, Professor Masaryk is a man of wide knowledge and intense culture; a man of exceptional brain power. He has studied the institutions of other countries, not only in books, but has made himself personally acquainted with the working of democracy in America and in England. He joins to his profound knowledge a nobility of character which makes him respected. His sincerity is beyond dispute. He has suffered long exile and other hardships for the cause to which he devoted himself. Nothing has ever spoiled his equable temperament, his love of justice, his passion for order, his demand for honest dealings, and his desire for peace.

But let it be admitted that as an organiser he is theoretical rather than practical; let it be admitted that he works out in his private cabinet schemes which he does not himself apply. But he has a most admirable executive Minister in Dr. Benes, whose position is unique. Dr. Benes is an active little man who is ready at a moment's notice to run about Europe on the errands of Masaryk. He is a man of indefatigable energy, who, besides maintaining personal contact with most of the Prime Ministers and Presidents on the Continent, helps his friend and master in the formidable task of putting into effect the plans conceived by the President.

There has lately been a tendency to depreciate Dr. Benes. He was described in one newspaper as a fussy little man, whose mediocre talents have been magnified by the journalists. Now I am not disposed to claim more for Dr. Benes than he may deserve. He may or may not be a man of great initiative: he may or may not be a supreme statesman. But whatever one may think of him, it is surely obvious that he is precisely the right man in the right place in the right circumstances. He is the henchman of Masaryk, and as such, is all that could be desired. Masaryk is the mind, Benes is the hand. It is an ideal combination, and it is one which has produced the most extraordinary results.

The situation of Benes is fairly secure, because it does not depend upon the changing spirit of parliament. He is not liable to be thrown down for a mere whim, a mere passing expression of dissatisfaction which may have permanent consequences. He is dependent on the President alone and the President has learnt in a long and close friendship and collaboration to appreciate his faithfulness and his executive qualities. These two men have gone through fire and storm together; they have worked side by side for many years; they have now reaped the reward of their efforts. They may be considered to be inseparable, to be complementary. Therefore, while Masaryk remains, Benes will probably remain. Great is Masaryk and Benes is his prophet!

The President of the Republic of Czecho-Slovakia is elected for a term of seven years. The constitution provides that a President may not be re-elected, but an exception is made for the first President. This is tantamount to

asserting that Masaryk is elected for life.   It is a
fine tribute of a people's gratitude.

But Masaryk deserves it.   He incarnates the
potency of an idea.   He embodies the spirit of a
people which, though composed of divers elements, became conscious of its nationality, and,
long before the war, strove for independence.
He is the true representative of patriotism—
patriotism that will not bow down to an alien
power which has obtained an apparently un-
shakable domination.   Masaryk is surely without ambition, for it would have been folly to
have cherished the ambition of becoming President of a State which was absorbed in and controlled by the great Austro-Hungarian Empire.
But it is not ambition that leads to high situation; it is rather the unswerving service of a
cause which appears to be a lost cause.   When
the cause is triumphant, those who have fought
for it, should, if th re is any justice and gratitude in the world, also be triumphant.

Masaryk is now seventy-four years of age.
He began his life in humble circumstances.   He
was apprenticed to a locksmith and then worked
as a blacksmith.   He found opportunities for
culture.   His scholarship is immense.   He be-

came professor of philosophy. He learnt many languages. He studied methods of government.

In 1878 he married an American woman, and his middle name—Garrigues—is her name which he incorporated in his own.

One thing which stood him in great stead is his Slovakian origin. Had he been a Czech it is possible that the Slovaks would not have been so willing to link their lot to the Czechs. As it is, the Czechs owe him their independence and the Slovaks are assured that minorities will always be properly represented. Even the Germans, who might have been a thorn in the side of the republic, have the greatest respect for the President and realise that they are members of a prosperous and comparatively happy community which has a great industrial future. The amalgamation is as complete as it well may be.

It was in the early part of the war that Masaryk, escaping from the dual monarchy, whose yoke had never been accepted, raised abroad the banner of revolt. The querulous criticism, which demands why a portion of the population of Austro-Hungary should be treated as allies instead of as enemies, is perfectly unjustified, for it was long before the outbreak of

the war that a group of patriots denounced the
oppression of their taskmasters. They did not
wait until the issue of the war was in sight before
throwing in their lot with the Allies.

In the end it was undoubtedly due to the
natural break-up of the ramshackle Empire,
provoked by the defection of Bohemia, that the
German and Austrian armies were defeated.
The Allies clearly owe a debt of gratitude to this
nation, as they owe a debt of gratitude to the
Poles. One may doubt whether the Balkanisa-
tion, as it has been called, of Central Europe,
will ultimately prove to make for peace and
stability. One may doubt the durability of
some of the new geographical demarcations.
But although it is possible to question some of
the details of the peace; although it is possible
even to question the principles of the peace;
it would have been, in practice, difficult to have
behaved otherwise than to give their freedom
to those who had done so much to win it.

Those who regard Bohemia as a natural part
of the German and Austrian system, which
luckily escaped in time to receive special treatment, are unacquainted with the dolorous history of the country. The Bohemian writers

filled their works with cries of despair and of choler. The Czech language was kept alive. There was a particular cult for Prague, and its great University, in which Masaryk taught. Prague was their capital and not Vienna or Budapest. In that wonderful city, with its pointed turrets and gables, its bizarre balconies, its antique roofs, its picturesque steeples, its acacias, in that beautiful city, the hope of release from the oppressor was cherished. But Czecho-Slovakia is not merely one of the seats of learning of Europe: it is also one of the most highly industrial regions of Europe, and its people are hard-working. At Pilsen are the great Skoda works. The Bohemian glass works employ many thousands of people. Textiles are produced in great quantities. Beet sugar is manufactured on a large scale. There is plenty of coal; there are great forests; there is an intensive agriculture. And Czecho-Slovakia is not only practically self-supporting but is able to export 75 per cent of its manufactured goods.

It is true that it is far from the sea—in spite of the Shakespearian blunder of "the seaboard of Bohemia"—but it has ports on the Danube and can obtain access to the sea by way of the

Elbe; while its railways are well-organised. Economically, the little country is certainly the strongest state in Europe.

But the attention of Masaryk was not only turned to the building up of a strong economic state. That is not sufficient. If it is to live, its political relations with its neighbours must be friendly. It must provide against attempts to overthrow the treaties. That has been the principal preoccupation of Masaryk. In the first place, he was bound to come to terms with the other beneficiaries of the various treaties, and it was not long before what is called the Little Entente was constructed. The Little Entente has for object the strict observation of the treaties. It may, therefore, be said, not unfairly, to be directed more or less pointedly against possible Hungarian aggression. Hungary, reduced to the smallest proportions, the seat of a proud and warlike people, may, it is thought, one day resort to arms to reacquire some of her lost territory.

Therefore, it was obvious that it was to the interest of Czecho-Slovakia to have an understanding with Rumania and with Yugo-Slavia, and, to some extent, with Poland. And this was perfectly legitimate; but the danger was that the once oppressed states should in turn seek to oppress the former oppressor and try to hold down Hungary too rigorously. At first this danger appeared to be real; but recently, under the wise guidance of Masaryk, the greatest aid has been given to Hungary, to raise loans, to restore her finances, and to consolidate herself in Central Europe.

This meant the release of the liens held in respect of reparations. It would have been too much to expect that the Little Entente could have consented to this course without some kind of protest, without some kind of struggle, without some kind of guarantees. But that in the end the Little Entente agreed is a striking example of the sagacity of the Czecho-Slovakian President—for Czecho-Slovakia is unquestionably the leader of the Little Entente—and the genuine desire which exists in Central Europe for better relations.

It is imperative in the interests of peace and of trade that the new nations and the new-old nations should live together in amity.

Austria had already been saved from ruin and her reparation debts practically wiped out.

When one considers the resistance which was put up by certain of the greater Allies to a reasonable arrangement with Germany, one will see that commonsense is not a prerogative of the greater powers, but that the smaller powers of Europe have set an example which augurs well for the future of the world.

It was at one time thought that Austria would ineluctably join up with Germany, and this would have been a menace to Czecho-Slovakia. But countries respond to kindly treatment, and it is sincerely to be hoped that all the little nations will form a happy family along the Danube.

There is also the threat of Russian aggression on Rumania, who has added Bessarabia to her possessions; but even this threat appears to have largely vanished. Czecho-Slovakia is encouraging good relations with the great neighbour of the North, and the Slavs and semi-Slavs should exist side by side in peace. With Italy, the Jugo-Slavs have made a pact, and from this side, too, there seems to be nothing now to fear.

There remains, however, the problem of Germany. France quickly saw the advantage—or supposed advantage—of constructing alliances, both with Poland and with Czecho-Slovakia. A few months ago President Masaryk came to Paris and laid the foundations of a treaty with France. There was considerable misgiving in western countries. England, particularly, was alarmed. Had Czecho-Slovakia, under the leadership of President Masaryk, finally decided to throw in her lot with France and form a link in a chain of nations from the Baltic to the Black Sea which would be ready to bear upon Germany at any moment at the bidding of France?

For my part, I think there has been much exaggeration. The treaty with France is a perfectly natural one and implies no hostility toward any other nation in Europe. It is purely defensive; purely designed to preserve existing treaties.

The last thing that President Masaryk wants is to be engaged in warfare of any kind. The whole interests, the whole prospects of Czecho-Slovakia, lie in the preservation of peace. This is true of all other countries, but of none is it so obviously and indisputably true as of Czecho-Slovakia. Here is a tiny state with an abnormally long frontier to defend. Whichever way the fortunes of war went in any conflict in Central Europe, Czecho-Slovakia would almost certainly be overrun. She would be in danger of extinction. Moreover, Czecho-Slovakia is built upon the foundations of international trade. I have already pointed out that she can export 75 per cent of her manufactured goods. This is an extremely important fact, for if a country which depends upon trade finds the complicated machinery of international relations shattered, it suffers not only momentarily as does a purely agricultural country, but permanently. In a word, Masaryk has based all his hopes on the continuance of peace in Europe. He has seen that only in the solidarity of the Continent, in the growing interdependence of peoples, has his country a certainty of survival.

That is why Dr. Benes is one of the most active and earnest workers for the League of Nations; for in the League of Nations, and all that it involves, in the principles of arbitration, of open diplomacy, of free communications, of mutual friendliness, of peace, lies the supreme hope of Czecho-Slovakia.

IV

MONSIEUR MILLERAND, who was elected President of the French Republic in 1920 in the place of M. Deschanel, whose health had given way under the strain, is a vigorous, square-shouldered, shock-headed man, who gives you the impression above all of enormous strength. That is, indeed, his supreme quality, mentally and physically. He is essentially a healthy man.

He is, as the Scotch say, a little slow on the up-take; he is by no means subtle; he has none of the reputed qualities of the French. He is not volatile, lively, imaginative—in a word, French. He is, on the contrary, calm, dogged—in a word, British.

These attempts to attribute characteristics to nations are entirely mistaken. There is no such thing as a French character in reality. The French, like the British, and like the Americans,

49

are composed of all sorts and conditions of men. Indeed, France, as we now know it, is an amalgamation of many races, and the stolid, dogmatic, quietly self-assertive M. Millerand is, in spite of his dissimilarity from the popular conception of the Frenchman, by no means a unique figure.

M. Millerand looks what he is: sturdy, cautious, tenacious, patient, a hard worker, with an infinite capacity for taking pains, methodical, plodding, never striving for brilliance, suspicious of cleverness that flaunts itself. He is intensely loyal, as he has shown over and over again during his political career.

When he was War Minister, for example, during the early part of the war, it was obvious that his subordinates were making bad blunders in respect of armament. The wrong kind of guns were being supplied; munitions were lacking; the French authorities, like most army authorities, were reluctant to change their traditional ways. They could not adapt themselves to the new conditions of modern warfare. Their slow minds would not allow them to abandon outworn theories. They were attacked in Parliament time after time, and M. Millerand,

to use the French phrase, covered them, refused to censure them, to change them, or per-
suade them to adopt more up-to-date methods.

Whether this kind of faithfulness to subordinates is good or bad in a time of crisis, may
be open to discussion, but one is bound to admire
the man who, in the face of Parliament, sticks
up for those who are under him, declines to be
browbeaten, or to allow those who are responsible for the conduct of his department to be
personally attacked.

He took the full responsibility himself, and it
must be confessed that his reputation suffered.
But we all have the defects of our qualities and
every quality has its defects. There is something in the steadiness, the reliability of M.
Millerand that is good for France, and M.
Millerand was sent to the Elysée just because
he had given a striking example of his capacity
for sticking to his point in face of any opposition.

It will be remembered that when he was
Prime Minister in 1920 he staked his political
fortunes in the saving of Warsaw from the
Bolsheviks. Everybody else had given up
Warsaw. Mr. Lloyd George in England was
urging the Poles to surrender before a worse

fate should befall them. What was there, indeed, to stop the victorious sweep of the Red armies? The Polish armies were in retreat; utterly broken and routed. There was nothing to stop the victorious sweep of the Red armies—except M. Millerand.

Against all reason, against all warning, against the opinion of the whole world, M. Millerand declared that he would not desert the Poles, that he would not permit a triumph of Bolshevism. All the cleverer statesmen looked aghast: M. Millerand was not only committing political suicide, but he was involving in his downfall the Polish nation, which would surely have been well advised to have surrendered.

He had already shown his contempt for nice speculations which would insure his being on the winning side. He had recognised the Wrangel Government when Wrangel was making his attack in Southern Russia against the Bolshevik forces. It was bad policy, if, indeed, it was a piece of policy at all. The truth is that M. Millerand was obliged to assert himself, to translate his feelings into acts. Any diplomatist would have declared without hesitation that the recognition of Wrangel was a stupend-

ous error, because diplomacy is in its nature
prudent and dislikes to run any risks. The risk
was not only great, but, in fact, M. Millerand
lost heavily when Wrangel was defeated and
overthrown.

Surely, this should have taught M. Millerand
a lesson; it should surely have persuaded him
that he must not gamble again; that he must be
more careful, and place himself on the winning
side, not on the losing side, without such regard
to loyalties. But M. Millerand was incorrigible;
he had learnt no lesson except the lesson of
loyalty which had stood him in such bad stead.

Once more he declared war against Bolshevism, precisely at the moment when Bolshevism
had Warsaw in its grasp. With remarkable
coolness, disregarding all advice, he sent General
Weygand to take charge of the Polish armies,
to make a final rally against the Red armies,
He was just in time: something like a miracle
happened. Warsaw was saved; the Poles recovered their courage, their forces were reorganised, Bolshevism was checked. M. Millerand
had his reward. He became the hero of the
French nation. It is of course nonsense to
describe him as the only statesman in Europe

who at this critical moment showed real foresight. He showed no foresight whatever; he only showed indomitable courage: he only displayed the doggedness of his character.

Sometimes loyalty is far better than reason. It was so on this occasion, and Mr. Lloyd George, who had counselled surrender, was wrong, while M. Millerand, who had insisted on the necessity of resistance to the end, was right. The French people, who respect strength perhaps more than any other people, unanimously asked M. Millerand to accept the Presidency of the French Republic which had then fallen vacant.

Now this incident, to which I have referred at some length, gives the key to the character of M. Millerand. He is a four-square man, with a square face, square chin, square shoulders, square fists and square body. His grey hair is like a lion's mane, but his whole aspect is that of a bull dog, who, having once taken hold, will never let go. Certainly he was cleverly caught time after time by the more agile Mr. Lloyd George, but the more agile Mr. Lloyd George in the long run was beaten, as he was bound to be beaten, by the stern, resolute M. Millerand.

With this inflexibility, this spirit of perseverance, this rather slow-moving resolution, M. Millerand is one of the most likable of men. One takes him for the family man *par excellence.* Even at the Elysée he has retained his simple habits. He is perfectly accessible to anybody who has a real excuse for endeavouring to penetrate into the presidential precincts. He not only receives readily, but he puts his visitors immediately at their ease. He converses even with strangers in the most familiar manner. He discusses politics precisely as though he were discussing politics with his neighbour in a Paris café. He is affable and certainly not secretive.

One passes through a series of rooms in which work military attachés and civilian secretaries before reaching the sanctum of the President, and as one passes through room after room there is a long line of bowing figures. The contrast after this ceremonious progress with the plain, unaffected President must have struck many of his casual visitors.

He has a few "intimates," old cronies, with whom he is happy to pass his evenings. Among them is Marshal Foch, and the two old cronies love to while away the time with a game of dominoes. Naturally, they do not allow less important affairs to interfere with the game, but one wonders whether these domino parties did not help to revive the demand for the fixing of the German frontier at the Rhine and the occupation of the Ruhr rather from the strategic point of view than from the point of view of reparations.

Everybody in these days has begun to suspect that political events are often decided by the most trivial accidental causes, and it is indeed possible—though I do not put it forward as a fact—that recent political history was considerably influenced by the common liking of Millerand and Foch for a game of dominoes.

But M. Millerand does indeed, in many ways, remind one of the café politician, in spite of the state with which he is surrounded. He likes to meet his friends for a chat; and he likes, above all, the comfort and kindliness of the home. In a country where it has become fashionable to have no family, M. Millerand is the happy, smiling paterfamilias, the centre of a family group. His son, Jean Millerand, indeed, acted as his secretary at the Elysée.

M. Millerand is distinctly not a President who is always on duty. His predecessor, M.

Deschanel, an exceedingly able and accomplished man, was always on duty. He took his task with excessive seriousness. He accepted every invitation to preside over every little banquet, to open every little exhibition, that was showered upon him. He had regularly four or five little discourses to recite in a day. As he used to write these speeches, even with secretarial assistance, he was kept going all the time. Towards the end of his short career as President, he was obviously overworked. He confessed as much to me the last time I saw him. "It is dreadful," he said, "I never have a moment to spare, never a moment to myself."

His pockets crammed with discourses, it is not surprising that he should on one occasion have pulled out the wrong manuscript and proceeded to read a speech which was altogether inapplicable. The poor man, with his desire to be ubiquitous, to refuse nobody, to make himself popular, quickly wore himself down, and the result was that his nerves and his brain gave way. He fell in a moment of aberration, from a railway train which was taking him to one of the innumerable functions he had promised to attend.

Now, M. Millerand is an altogether different type of man. He is a real worker, but he is not likely to overstrain himself. While performing all his duties, he has taken care not to overload himself with the more negligible functions of the presidential life. Anyhow, his physical power is tremendous. He is strong enough to fell an ox, and if such a feat were part of his presidential functions, he would doubtless perform it admirably. When he was proposed as President, it was his physical vigour which made a special appeal to the French. They had had enough of sickly candidates. "A man who can eat a beefsteak, that is the sort of President we want," said somebody to me at the time. France wanted no more "histories." She had had enough of scandals and misfortunes: she wanted a great, hearty countryman, who would be placid.

And yet, strangely enough, ponderous as M. Millerand appeared to be, there was a probability time after time of another presidential crisis. For M. Millerand had an idea, and when M. Millerand has an idea, he does not easily forget it. His idea was that the French President has not enough power. French Presidents,

unlike American Presidents, have no effective
power. Every act must be approved by a Minister; every message or document of any kind
must be countersigned by a Minister. Now,
there have been many Presidents in France who
have endeavoured to break away from the
limitations imposed upon them, but they always
had to resign themselves to the inevitable consequences of the constitution, or have been broken
as President MacMahon was broken. With a
strong Prime Minister the President is helpless.
M. Poincaré discovered this to his deep chagrin
when M. Clemenceau was Prime Minister: and
M. Millerand discovered this to his chagrin when
M. Poincaré was Prime Minister.

But, at any rate, M. Millerand put up a gallant fight. When he was elected, he put forward as a condition of his acceptance his right
to control the general policy of France and thus
preserve continuity. Nobody agreed to this
condition; nobody had the right to agree to this
condition: but it may be that M. Millerand,
having made his declaration, was justified in
believing that it was implicitly agreed to.

While a President is popular and has exceptional prestige, he may indeed be predominant,

but that he can ever hope to choose his Prime
Ministers, and that these Prime Ministers will
consent to be his mere instruments, is a fantastic fancy. At any rate, M. Millerand tried. M.
Leygues was his first Prime Minister and M.
Leygues was obliged to accept his Cabinet
ready-made from the hands of M. Millerand.
Then came M. Briand and M. Briand is too
slippery to be controlled. When at Cannes M.
Briand appeared to be giving away French
rights and departing from the line traced by M.
Millerand, the President sent him a telegram
which brought him back helter-skelter to Paris
and compelled him to resign.

That was perhaps the first notable intervention of M. Millerand in foreign affairs. But he
was always hankering after real control, and
even with M. Poincaré, tried often, through
inspired newspaper statements and through
personal protests, to direct the course of events.
So much so, that there was for a long time much
coolness between the President and the Prime
Minister.

M. Poincaré, speaking out of bitter experience, reminded M. Millerand that the capital
fact about French Presidents is that they are

irresponsible. Now responsibility must accompany power. If a President who cannot be checked in any way by Parliament, who cannot be removed from office, who cannot be called to account for his actions, were to do as he pleases, he would become a Dictator. Parliament would count for nothing. In truth, M. Millerand seemed to aspire to this rôle of Dictator, and there were at one period persistent rumours that General Mangin had been sounded, not of course by the President but by over-zealous friends, on the possibility of repeating in another form the coup of Mussolini.

We must have a Dictator, cried morning after morning the "Victoire" of M. Gustave Hervé, who has in recent years passed for the particular mouthpiece of M. Millerand. But M. Poincaré stood firm. He would not admit that a revision of the constitution was an urgent matter. He would not permit M. Millerand to address a message to Parliament as he wished to do in March, 1924. M. Millerand had to be content with addressing a message to the country through the medium of the "Matin"—which, while making clear that it emanated from the President, did not dare to attach his name to it directly. In this message, however, it was plainly intimated that M. Millerand might resign if the elections went against the Bloc National, and the policy which he had initiated in 1920 were reversed. This was, indeed, a serious threat. Immediately there was much speculation on the possibility of M. Millerand's escape from the presidential prison-house into active political life.

Who would be his successor if he chafed too much in his helpless position? There was no doubt in the minds of many men that in a sudden presidential crisis it would be M. Poincaré who would be put back in the Elysée.

It is hard to think of M. Millerand as a revolutionary, but this peace-loving, stalwart man has not only shown signs of wishing to make a revolution de Palais but in his early career was a revolutionary of the Left. Many French politicians have "evolved." He began as a Socialist. His audacity was remarkable. Particularly did he fight against Boulanger, who was accused of a Cæsarian policy. Is it not odd that the ardent youth, who was the enemy of Boulangism, should to-day in his turn be suspected of Cæsarism?

But there is a whole series of antitheses to make about M. Millerand. Thus it was in 1896 that he proclaimed at Saint-Mandé the right to strike, and in 1920 not only smashed the great strike but broke up the French amalgamation of trade unions, known as the Confédération Générale du Travail.

Thus he played a notable part in the anti-Clerical legislation and the liquidation of the "congregations," but (whirligig of years!) it was under his Government that there began negotiations for the re-establishment of diplomatic relations with Rome. One should not regard the lives of politicians too closely; one should not search for inconsistencies; for times change and politicians with time. Did not most of us begin as radicals and end up in middle life as conservatives, if not as reactionaries? Why refuse to the professional politician the right of development that we claim for ourselves?

One day at the beginning of the Presidency of M. Millerand, when I was presiding over a luncheon given in his honour, I asked him if he did not feel the wear and tear of office. "No," he replied, "I never let things worry me." That, after all, is the secret of M. Millerand's strength. He is a hard worker, a cheerful family man: he has strong ideas which he endeavours to put into practice; he seeks rather than shrinks from responsibility, but he never worries. Therein lies his strength.

NOTE.—The French elections have since been held and the Radicals, with the support of the Socialists, on May 11, unexpectedly came into power. Their first act was to force the resignation of M. Millerand and to elect, on June 13, M. Doumergue to the Elysée.

V

UNDOUBTEDLY the dominating figure in the finances of Europe for the past few years, that is to say, the decisive years since the war, has been Sir John Bradbury.

The newspapers speak of him from time to time, but he has never received the attention that should have gone to one who has so directed the course of events. It is probably true that the public does not interest itself particularly in finance. It looks rather to the politicians. It inquires very seriously what manner of men are the politicians, but it does not inquire what manner of men are the financial advisers who, after all, shape the policy of our modern world. Nobody has shaped policy more than Sir John Bradbury.

He has been the *éminence grise* not of one

British Prime Minister but of at least five. They have consulted him above all on the problems of reparations, and if England took a certain line of action, it was because men might come and men might go in the British Government, but Sir John Bradbury went on forever. He was always at the elbow of the Prime Minister, giving him counsel which the Prime Minister invariably accepted. Sir John Bradbury was originally one of Asquith's men. He was appointed head of the British Treasury as a young man—the youngest man who has ever occupied that supreme post.

During the war his signature was on the paper One Pound Treasury Notes which circulated instead of golden sovereigns. Bradbury was responsible for the financing of the war, and he fulfilled his task with amazing ability. He was afterwards a powerful influence in the shaping of the finances of peace.

It was his principle of maintaining British credit at all costs which was adopted and which has been the basis of all subsequent British policy. British financial policy, by which all other policy is conditioned, can be summed up in a few words—the pound must not be allowed

to depreciate. It was for this reason that at the
price of a terrible hardship England paid a
larger proportion of the expense of war out of
current revenue than any other of the belliger-
ents. It was for this reason that taxation was
screwed up to the highest pitch. It was for this
reason that England decided not to take any
risk of Germany not paying the tremendous sums
demanded from her in reparations, but preferred
to regard reparations, if they were made, rather
as a windfall that should not in the meantime
be reckoned in the budget. It was for this
reason that England, unlike France, balanced
her budgets and did not report to the device
of a second budget of so-called Recoverable Ex-
penditure.

The German debt was quickly discounted.
This was undoubtedly sound finance from a
certain point of view, but it inevitably directed
British policy into a different path from that
which France had taken. The ways divided.
France, with her budget of Recoverable Expen-
diture, was obliged to believe in the possibility
of reparations, and the longer the budget was
kept in existence, the longer France's hopes were
disappointed, the more complete and hopeless

became the muddle unless, in fact, Germany did pay, and the more determined France naturally became that Germany should be made to pay.

The British, on the other hand, in accordance with the theories of Sir John Bradbury, in accordance with the guiding principle of their finance, having wiped out for practical purposes their credits on Germany, became somewhat indifferent to German payments, cherished no illusions, and at last became active partisans of the doctrine that it was folly to expect any important sums from Germany, and that France, therefore, by persisting in her course of coercion was wrecking the peace of Europe and destroying the potential prosperity of the Continent. Moreover, the hostility towards France which developed from the opposing financial conceptions, was intensified by the economic result in England, which might have been foreseen. This economic result was the loss of trade and the corresponding increase of unemployment.

Either the general aim of Europe should have been to maintain the national currencies at something like the pre-war level, or the agreed policy should have been the general depreciation

of moneys. But when on the one hand you had
a great nation which lived on its industries and
on its foreign markets, striving to keep the
pound as high as the dollar, and on the other
hand, you had practically all the continental
countries, which might have been markets for
Great Britain, allowing their currencies to drop
to a third, a fourth, a tenth part of the pre-war
value, then it was clear that in the economic
sense the country that would suffer most would
be precisely the country which had the high
currency.

The medium of exchange was smashed: wages
had not risen: the general standard had not been
raised as expressed in francs or lire as quickly
as the franc and the lira had fallen. The consequence was that France, for example, with
depreciated money could manufacture much
more cheaply than England with relatively appreciated money, and could sell her productions
even in the British market itself, whereas the
British could certainly not sell their goods priced
in pounds to the French and to the other peoples
of Europe.

It should not necessarily be suggested that the
British were wrong in theory, but in the world

in which there must be give and take, a compromise in practice, in a world in which the other nations were not following the example of England, the effect on trade was disastrous. At one time no fewer than two million workers in England were without employment. They had to be provided for. What is known as the dole was instituted, and so high was the dole that a number of ne'er-do-wells preferred to receive the dole for doing no work than to work, even were work to be found, for comparatively little more pay.

It has been calculated that in one way or another, directly or indirectly, the British authorities have paid away on unemployment as much as 400 million pounds, or, roughly, two milliard dollars. In the meantime, France was economically prosperous. There was work for everybody; indeed, foreign labour had to be imported.

We have already seen that the British people had been led away from the idea of reparations, and had been taught to regard the French as improvident, illogical, and unreasonable. There had been the most pointed reference to the French system of relying upon reparations for budgetary purposes, while the British were

compelled to pay 5s. in the pound—that is
to say 25 per cent—in income tax alone. But
the British felt themselves to be still more
unfairly treated, still more heavily burdened,
when they looked upon their devastated regions—that is to say, their unemployment—
and compared them to the French devastated
regions which, at any rate, were providing employment.

It will be seen, therefore, on this exceedingly
summary statement of the case, that the French
and British objectives were entirely different;
were, indeed, diametrically opposed. It will
be seen that while the French were more and
more compelled to seek reparations, the British
were turning more and more from reparations
as the solution of their difficulties; were regarding
reparations as the very cause of their difficulties;
and were asking instead that the search for
reparations should cease and that Europe should
settle down in peace, stabilise its moneys, open
its markets, and allow England once again to
become prosperous. All this unmistakably flows
from the original doctrine of keeping the pound
at par at any cost.

It will be said, however, that Sir John Bradbury was not at the Treasury during the development of the British policy. This is perfectly true, but he had given the impetus to British policy and, further, was the most powerful influence at the British Treasury, even when he was no longer there. He had acquired the most formidable legendary reputation in financial circles. The Treasury officials may be said to be his young men; they looked upon him as their master. Successive Prime Ministers consulted him, not only on the subject of reparations when he went as the British delegate to the Reparation Commission, but on the larger financial policy of Great Britain. Mr. Lloyd George had implicit faith in him, although Mr. Lloyd George was somewhat erratic in his diplomatic behaviour. Mr. Bonar Law accepted his advice unreservedly. Mr. Baldwin, even more of the city man than his predecessors, listened to Sir John Bradbury and to the Governor of the Bank of England, Mr. Montagu Norman, who may again be regarded as one of Sir John's pupils.

It was hardly possible for Mr. Ramsay Macdonald, coming into a situation that had long been created and consolidated, to do otherwise than take heed of the counsels of the Nestor of British finance—though Sir John is, if the paradox be allowed—a young Nestor.

Sir John Bradbury had been early sent to the Reparation Commission. The choice was perhaps not the most fortunate one, if one considers the whole of the circumstances. Of the remarkable efficiency, the superlative talent of Sir John Bradbury, there could be no question—indeed, after discussing these subjects with Sir John almost daily for several years, I have come to the conclusion that there is no abler man in his particular sphere to be found—but the point is that having helped to put British financial policy on certain definite lines, he could scarcely be an impartial judge of Germany's capacity to pay. His judgment was bound to be warped by his preconceived ideas. He was bound to regard the problem of reparations in the light of the whole British financial system, and to take up what could only be an anti-French attitude. An anti-French attitude meant that Germany would be encouraged to escape if possible from her engagements. It meant that sooner or later Germany would imagine that England was on her side and

France would imagine that England was on the side of Germany.

Thus began the tug of war that has brought about the upheaval of Europe and that has kept America for so long out of the European world. In all this neither France nor England has been particularly to blame. The outcome has been merely the logical outcome of the premises adopted and the premises in themselves on either side have much to commend them.

It might well be that, going further than Sir John Bradbury, the whole notion of reparations after the war was utterly wrong and could only lead to mischief—unless a reparation figure which Germany could have covered immediately had been fixed in 1919.

That Germany should pay reparations is, of course, just. The French insist on the justice of their case. But in practical life justice is not everything; it is also necessary to consider the possibilities. Now, in the first place, it seemed incredible that Germany, who had suffered more than any other belligerent country during the war and whose defeat was in fact due to the long food blockade, should be able to set her own house in order, while France and England

and even the United States, would find it difficult to do so, and in addition, pay tribute to the
victors. This idea seemed to suppose that the
Germans were a race of supermen, of far greater
capacity than Englishmen, Frenchmen, and
Americans. But apart from this obvious flaw
in allied reasoning, it was certain that Germany
would attempt to evade any obligations imposed upon her. The French have always
expressed the utmost astonishment that Germany should have shown bad faith. Surely,
much more astonishment would have been called
for had Germany shown good will.

Without pretending to know what was in
the mind of Sir John Bradbury, it may be stated
as a simple fact that Sir William Goode, who
was at the head of the Austrian section of the
Commission of Reparations, deliberately went
out to torpedo his section. He did not believe—
and he was undoubtedly right—in the capacity
of Austria to pay reparations, he gradually
convinced his colleagues, and went out to assist
Austria instead of making demands on Austria,
and is to-day performing a similar task on behalf
of Hungary, on whom high reparation demands
were made. Now, although the circumstances

are not the same, there is nevertheless a certain similarity between Austria, Hungary, and Germany. Does Sir John wish to torpedo the Reparation Commission?

The real cause of misunderstandings on the Reparation Commission, where Sir John Bradbury was always in a minority, was perhaps psychological. Sir John, the honest Englishman with sound traditional financial conceptions, could not believe in French calculations; could, indeed, hardly conceal his contempt for French finance. It all appeared to him to be so hopelessly and helplessly wrong. He threw up his hands at the French budgetary system; he shook his head at the inadequate imposition of taxes in France; he raised his eyebrows at the French computations regarding Germany's capacity. He could not restrain a chuckle at the fall of the franc, for it demonstrated the accuracy of his predictions.

To tell the truth, Sir John found himself in more senses than one in a foreign country, and did not disguise his surprise that anybody should think differently from himself and the British Treasury. He was precisely like those English and American visitors to Paris who grow some-

what indignant because the shopkeepers speak
an alien tongue. He looked down upon the
French with some pity; sometimes he patronised
them and behaved with the greatest good humour; but always he despised them. He would
admit that they made the prettiest compli-
mentary speeches and were subtle in their
diplomatic methods, but what were these things
beside their dark ignorance of modern credit
and banking rules? So it came about that this
fine type of Englishman, insular, not accessible
to foreign ideas, dogmatic on those subjects
which he undoubtedly best knew, became for the
French, without intending to be so, somewhat
prickly.

If only there had been greater attempts to
reconcile some of the French formulas with the
British formulas, it could have been done. But
neither side would change the exact terms of
their arguments. In the end it was clear that
Sir John Bradbury was fighting against the
French. He was even opposed to the Rathenau
offer of 750 million gold marks as the 1922 payments. This offer was made at Cannes and Sir
John found it too high.

As a man, there is nobody I have ever known

who is more likable than Sir John Bradbury, but it takes an Englishman, or perhaps an American, to understand him. He is careless about all that does not touch his particular task. His personal appearance is, for example, quite a matter of indifference. His hair is ragged: his clothes are ill-worn. There is told a story of how he met an old school friend at Cannes, whom he had not seen for ten years. "You are looking exactly the same," said the friend, "you have not changed a bit; you are even wearing the same clothes." But this anecdote only serves to emphasise the utter devotion to duty of Sir John, his absorption in his work which he performs with a single eye to the service of his country. Sir John is the best kind of civil servant that England possesses: scrupulous, conscientious, utterly incapable of taking advantage of his knowledge for the furtherance of his own fortunes, but also incapable of conceding any point to those whom he would consider to be the adversaries of his ideas and of his country.

VI

LYAUTEY: FRENCH EMPIRE BUILDER

We do not sufficiently define our terms. When France is accused of being imperialistic, the suggestion apparently is that she wishes to extend her dominion in Europe. In that sense the accusation is untrue. But if by imperialism one means the spreading abroad of French influence in dark places, the colonisation of great tracks of uncivilised land, then France is undoubtedly imperialistic, precisely as England and, in her own way, America are.

The great imperialist is Marshal Lyautey. He is only one of a number of men who are working for the expansion of France—in Africa, in the Near East, in the Far East and in various scattered territories. But he seems to sum up and centralise the new French movement.

He is the greatest of the empire builders and his example has inspired others. Were it not for the success of the Moroccan adventure—one might almost call it the Moroccan miracle—the French would probably have remained a home-staying people,—taking no interest in a France overseas, hugging their frontiers around them, satisfied with the prison walls of their geographical configuration. For the French are not travellers, they are not enterprising.

In their blood is the blood of the Romans who, from their city spread out far and wide, who knew the whole world as it was to be known and who conquered the greater part of it and civilised it. But the French seemed to have lost these Roman virtues. They took little interest in their possessions, they became insular, they disliked voyages, they were anything but colonisers.

All this is changed. There is in France a band of very enthusiastic imperialists—that is to say, men who strive to make the most of the countries submitted to French rule, men who wish to foster a popular interest in a greater France. They appear to be succeeding admirably. There is indeed much popular interest in France in the colonies and protectorates. And in the colonies and protectorates themselves im-

provements are being effected with remarkable
speed. Large countries have been transformed
and the transformation is nowhere so surprising
as it is in Morocco.

"France a country with a declining birth-
rate! The French a decaying people!" cried
Marshal Lyautey. "But France has not, as you
suppose, a population of less than forty millions.
It is a vast domain of at least 100 million inhabitants."

That is the keynote of the new France. It
would be folly to ignore this salient point. If I
could convey an impression of the innumerable
schemes of irrigation in desert regions, of railways to run through wild forests, of motor-roads
to be built across mountains, of airplane services
to fly across continents; if I could convey an
impression of the multiplicity of plans that have
been formed and that in some cases have received
the serious beginnings of execution, the reader
would appreciate what is obvious to the foreign
observer living in France—that France is a
country of immense energy which needs new out-
lets and which is finding them, particularly in
Northern Africa.

There are territories which have been under

French control much longer than Morocco. Morocco is, so far as the French are concerned, new. Algeria and Tunis begin to be old. But it is nevertheless Morocco which has given the impetus to French colonisation, and it is Marshal Lyautey, the maker of modern Morocco, who stands up head and shoulders above other French colonisers. When most of the statesmen of whom we talk today have long been forgotten, the name of Lyautey will be held in higher honour than ever. He typifies the new France; he has not only in a remarkably short space of time conquered and pacified and developed a rich region which will add largely to the national wealth, but he has moved the whole nation. He is indirectly—indeed, why not say, directly—responsible for the acquisition of other lands in Africa right down beyond the Equator, and their better utilisation. He is responsible, too, for the development of Indo-China, and all other parts in which French influence has exerted itself in the interests of a higher civilisation.

It is his romantic figure which has stirred not only the people, but the rulers of the people. Lyautey is a striking instance of the right man in the right place. Nobody else could have done with Morocco what he has done, and it is probable that in another capacity Lyautey would have been a failure. During the war his fame was so great that at a critical moment he was taken away from Morocco and made War Minister in France. The result was deplorable. The soldier, who had shown himself to be a statesman of the highest kind in Morocco, did not know the elementary rules of parliamentary life in the metropolis. He provoked indignation and anger by frank statements which it is not the proper thing to make, even in war time, in France.

His resignation quickly came. He went back to Morocco, from whence he should never have been brought. He went back a failure in the unaccustomed task which had been imposed upon him, but he went back undiminished in stature. Everybody realised that his rôle is a bigger rôle than that of the politician. He is the soldier, the ruler of subject races. When he issues a proclamation in Morocco, it is exactly what it should be. It makes the precise impression intended. When he utters a ministerial statement in the French Parliament, he finds himself speaking to men who talk, as it were, another language. He understands the Moroccans better than he understands the French.

In my personal relations with Marshal Lyautey I found him a particularly likable man in spite of his haughtiness and irritability. He is a fine, tall, upstanding figure of a soldier, with an open, intelligent countenance, the strong nose of a conqueror, magnificent mustache, and a shortcropped, brush-like, square head of white hair.

Even when in his Paris home, in an old picturesque house, in an old narrow street, on the left bank of the river, he maintains himself in state. Around the courtyard are the smaller flats of humbler folk, who are astonished on his rare visits to Paris to see gorgeous keepers of the door. In his salon there are wonderfully apparelled chieftains. His suite is always with him. He maintains his household as the Governor even when he is at home.

There is no doubt that he has grown to like pomp and display. Most Frenchmen are willing to drop the show of power, the circumstance of their situation; but not so Marshal Lyautey. It has become part of his life. It has unquestionably served its purpose, and the splendour which he affects is more than excusable, it is essential.

Rumours of his impending retirement came from time to time but one could only receive them with scepticism. How could Lyautey ever become a simple citizen again? But it must not be supposed that this grandeur was anything but one of the instruments which he used. It was not empty and hollow. Lyautey was a great military commander and he knew how to govern with skill and with discretion. The Sultan, though enjoying nominally sovereign rights in this protectorate, is, of course, a mere puppet. It is only a little more than twelve years ago that France obtained the protectorate by a treaty with the Sultan. Until that time the Moorish Government was an oriental despotism.

Not many years ago prisoners were mutilated and put in iron cages. There were even such barbarous spectacles as those of prisoners after a combat being torn to pieces by tigers. Now, although in Morocco there are still to be found most primitive conditions, there exist side by side with rush huts great tourist hotels of the most modern kind, splendid villas and all the appurtenances of civilisation as it is known in the big cities of the world.

In motor-cars, running over good roads, you will pass fields in which wooden plows turn up the soil. There are jazz bands in the cafés and outside snake charmers. There are Parisian frocks and there are Arabian and Berber robes. Everywhere the contrast between semi-barbaric customs and European manners impress the visitor. But everywhere in the French zone of Morocco there is a feeling of complete safety; there is a feeling of increasing prosperity.

What is perhaps most to be admired in Marshal Lyautey as Resident-General, is his encouragement of the artist, and his preservation of picturesque sites and native costumes. He has refused to make a clean sweep of a world which is not our world. On the contrary, he has endeavoured to preserve it, so far as it is not dangerous to Europeans. He has not tried to destroy the character of the country or the character of the inhabitants. He has even revived ancient trades and crafts, and the artistic treasures of Morocco have been multiplied.

Many arts which were dying out have been placed on a better footing. Europeans have been brought in to discover and revive the art of pottery and of weaving. Around Lyautey, as

the Resident-General, are writers who in colourful
accounts of the life of Morocco, have made the
protectorate known at home, and have, moreover, produced works of great literary value.
This is surely the best kind of propaganda. In
nothing has Lyautey shown himself to be a man
of vision more than in his friendship, not only
with the specialists, the technicians, the engin-
eers, the architects, but with the artists, the
literary men, the antiquarians, who have, thanks
to personal invitations, come to take an intense
interest in the old warring region and to induce
their compatriots to take an equal interest.

Lyautey has many of the traditional qualities
of the empire-maker, but his introduction of the
artist as empire-maker is unique. He has used
the sword, but he has also used the pen. He has
been the law-giver, but he has also been the art
inspirer. He has improved, but he has also preserved. He has not only introduced a commercial civilisation, but has fostered the arts.
Surely for these things he deserves the eulogies
which have been showered upon him by all who
have seen him at work!

Be it remembered that five of the twelve years
since Morocco became a protectorate were war

years.   Morocco was a hotbed of German in-
trigue, and it might well have been thought that
when the war broke out the task of Lyautey in
Morocco would become formidable.   The new
Constitution was of such recent date that a
revolt of the gravest kind seemed inevitable, and
it is true that Lyautey encountered the greatest
difficulties.   But when it was proposed to send
him more troops he refused them; indeed, he
contributed troops to the mother country which
was then fighting for its existence, and, with the
scantiest forces, by the exercise of truly remarkable generalship, not only held the posts which
were under his control, but obtained control of
others.   He was advised to retire from the
interior, but he knew his strength and he refused
to lower the French flag.

Morocco under Lyautey is indeed a model of
imperial enterprise.   France has bettered the lot
of the native.   There has been no oppression,
but in the real sense, only protection.   One has
only to compare what has happened in the
French zone with what has happened in the
Spanish zone to realise the wonderful accomplishment of Lyautey, who has been at once
firm, efficient and kindly in his methods.   His

diplomacy—for he is a supreme diplomatist in his own sphere—has been called the diplomacy of the smile. He made friends instead of enemies of the Moroccan chiefs. Those who rebelled were beaten and then shook hands with their conqueror. The Spanish, on the other hand, have inextricably entangled themselves in difficulties. They have suffered reverse after reverse. Army after army has been swallowed up in the quagmire of the Spanish zone, lost in a thicket from which there seems to be no way of escape.

Would France take over the Spanish zone and thus unify the country and have a still firmer footing on the Mediterranean? This is a question which is often asked, and the Spanish jealousy of France arises largely from the suspicion that France is merely awaiting the propitious moment when Spain shall be utterly weary to acquire possession of the northern zone.

France would, of course, like nothing better— on condition that the job which would be set her were not too difficult. Now, as the abandonment of Morocco by Spain would indicate the hopelessness of the attempt at pacification, France would not be eager to succeed Spain.

Lyautey has said the last word on this subject. "It is possible," he said, "that many years hence Spanish Morocco will drop like a ripe fruit into our lap. But if it were offered to us today we would have to refuse it. It is true that we have by systematic work obtained good results in our zone, but as I see it, the position in the Spanish zone has become such that it would require 100,000 men of our French troops to restore order."

This year there was an international settlement with regard to Tangiers, the disputed port on the Mediterranean. This port, which is a sort of recognised harbour of refuge in the turbulent Spanish zone, comes under international control, though nominally the sovereignty of the Sultan is maintained, and in reality the French are predominant and are the true masters of Tangiers. The terms of the settlement are of little consequence. What matters is not the precise composition of the various international governing bodies, but the fact that henceforth there is to be no more dispute. It will be possible, therefore, to construct a really important port at Tangiers on the great seaway from the west to the east.

France, chiefly owing to Marshal Lyautey, is again calling herself a Mediterranean power. It was on the shores of the Mediterranean that civilisation first came to birth. Afterward power winged its way westward to the North Sea and later the Atlantic and the Pacific Oceans were all-important. But now many of the interests of the world seem again to be centring upon the Mediterranean, the cradle of civilisation. The wheel may yet turn full circle, the struggle may become a Mediterranean struggle. That is why the occasional enthusiastic talk of a Latin alliance—a grouping of the Mediterranean powers, Spain, France, Italy and the rest—appears to be on the wrong track. There are too many conflicts of interest, the race for supremacy is too keen.

That race, again thanks to Lyautey, will probably be won outright by France. Her north African empire is immense. Indeed, one should call it her African empire, for it extends uninterruptedly to below the Equator.

French motor cars cross the huge Sahara, French airplanes fly from colony to colony. From Senegal come most of the native regiments of the French Army. There is an enormous wealth in man power and in natural products to be exploited. The north of Africa may be said to be as French as the south of Africa is British, and France is indulging in the highest hopes.

Although Marshal Lyautey has cultivated only his own garden he is undoubtedly the animator of all this immense movement. It is impossible for France to witness the prosperity of Morocco without seeking to increase the prosperity of Algeria, or Tunisia, and of all the mandated territories which lie further south.

The colour line is not drawn in France as in other countries, and there is not the slightest repugnance to admitting into the French Republic in its wider sense swarthy-skinned citizens. France, if all goes well, will not have to be regarded as a narrow geographical expression. France, like Britain—perhaps better than Britain, for the amalgamation of races will be more complete—must be thought of as an empire, the metropolitan country and the overseas colonies and protectorates forming an inseparable whole.

VII

GENERAL DON MIGUEL PRIMO DE RIVERA Y
ORBANEJA is and looks the military man. He
comes of a family of soldiers. It is by no accident that he is himself a soldier. He possesses
the temperament of the military man. There
are, of course, many soldiers of genius, or at least
of great intelligence, but Primo de Rivera is of
the type which is at once simple in its ideas and
expeditive in its actions. He judges without
knowledge and is dogmatic and *autoritaire*.

With his heavy oblong face, with its heavy
expression, it would be difficult to pretend that
the man who became Dictator in Spain is a man
of exceptional gifts. But at least he is patriotic.
When Spain appeared to be falling to pieces,
while the King amused himself at a fashionable
seaside resort, Primo de Rivera suddenly felt
that the hour had struck to take command.

He is surely not to be blamed. He behaved according to his convictions and indeed the shock was calculated to steady the rolling ship of State. But, unfortunately, he has not the calibre of a statesman and has made as many mistakes since September, 1923, as any of his predecessors in power. He cannot be expected to understand literature, for example, but when he exiled Miguel de Unamuno to the Canary Islands, he committed a fault which is as bad for the reputation of Spain as was the murder of Ferrer. He revealed, in a flash, not only the reactionary character of his coup d'état, not only his own reactionary temperament, but the reactionary character of modern Spain, the last refuge of a peculiarly outmoded Roman Catholic thought.

While the Roman Catholic Church is evolving towards greater liberalism, the spirit of the Inquisition still persists in Spain. This incident of the expulsion of the Rector of the University of Salamanca explains the weakness of Spain, which lives in another age. The world has long learnt to laugh at the Primo de Riveras, but in Spain they may still flourish—booted *piccaresque* tyrants with wooden swords, as d'Annunzio says—who have learnt nothing, who do not realise that intellect also plays its part, and that this part is far more important than the part of the strutting soldiers of Madrid.

How is the comparative impotence of Spain in world politics to be explained? The Spanish language is among those which are the most widely spoken and it would have seemed that Spanish influence was destined to remain as vigorous as ever. It has been pointed out by M. Albert Mousset that after the great war two different policies opposed each other in Spain. According to one group, the Moroccan policy ought to be developed. According to the other group, Morocco ought to be treated merely as a piece of international money for bargaining purposes. Spain could not choose between these conceptions. She has remained in Morocco but she has lost prestige; she has suffered reverses which have had their repercussions in internal politics.

For a moment Spain appeared to be seeking friendships among the western powers and consented to certain sacrifices with regard to Tangiers. But she purchased little good will and is scarcely looked upon as a rival or a friend by

any country in Europe. Spain, it will be remarked, by her geographical position, must
communicate with the Continent across France.
She also stands at the entry of the great Mediterranean water-way but has no effective control. She has never managed to place herself
in close relations with Italy.

Across the Atlantic look the young South
American republics with veneration for the
ancient country whose culture they have preserved. But instead of drawing tighter these
bonds, Spain appears to be only concerned in
throwing her manpower and her money into the
great Moroccan morass.

While political Spain hardly counts for much,
she has made a brilliant artistic and literary
recovery. There can be little doubt that, as Mr.
Valery Larbaud remarks, "Spain is perhaps the
foremost intellectual nation of our time." Surely, then, it was for Spain to cease striving for
material advantages, since her material forces
have diminished, and to present to the world
her triumphs in letters, in painting, in science,
and above all, in philosophy!

Spain has taken a considerable part in the
formation of the League of Nations. She was

the first neutral State to sit upon the Council of the League. If only Spain had been rightly governed, she would be regarded as a pattern to the rest of humanity. But instead of proudly displaying her intellectual victories, she has floundered in the stupidest militarism, and to save herself from the muddle, could do nothing better than give effective power to Primo de Rivera, who promptly endeavoured to suppress the independence of spirit shown by writers in the Spanish language.

In the Paris cabarets there is sung a satirical song concerning Alphonso XIII, two lines of which run as follows:

> Vedette at Deauville:
> Simple figurant at Madrid.

And, indeed, the King with his love of sports and of pleasure, does not appear to take an active part in politics. He appeared to accept the perilous adventure of the Dictatorship smilingly, indifferently. But perhaps his apparent indifference is deceptive. He is wiser than he seems. While he pretends that the political forces in Spain are in no way stimulated by him, in reality he plays one against the other and maintains the principle of monarchy above the vicissitudes of the battle between the civilian and the soldier, the army and the people.

He was probably well aware of the projected coup d'état by Primo de Rivera and connived at it on condition that the army should be loyal to the Crown. Alphonso has, in fact, staked his fortunes for the moment on the military and the ecclesiastical authorities as against the intellectuals and the Liberals of his country. The experiment may turn out to be disastrous; and when Primo de Rivera falls, it may be doubted whether the King can evolve rapidly enough in the opposite direction.

It would be folly to pretend that the Spanish Dictator has any remarkable qualities; it would be folly to attempt to compare him with Mussolini. There is no resemblance whatever, either in respect of his origins, or his personal value, or his historic rôle, or his success.

The Dictatorship was never accepted by the people. It is true that the Spanish press remained silent, but silence in this case did not give consent. In Spain Liberalism has always pursued a precarious existence. The liberty of the press and of speech has encountered all kinds of obstacles. It was impossible to express hostility to the army. The church pressed heavily upon the whole social life, and other cults were almost impossible. The Crown has identified itself with the restrictions imposed upon freedom, and although there has been an alternation of governments—Conservative Governments succeeding Liberal Governments—the difference of doctrine, as Señor Alomar, a former Member of Parliament, has stated, between the Liberal and the Conservative Parties, was hardly perceptible in practice. The Conservative Party was perhaps more brutal and more arbitrary in its repression, but many of the worst measures have been the work of the Liberal Party.

In 1917 there was a moment when the indignation of the country seemed ready to explode in a revolution. The army had become undisciplined. There existed what were called the Juntas; but in face of the menace, the army unreservedly placed itself on the side of authority. The price paid for this intervention was terrible. The pressure of the army on Spanish policy has been most conscious and constant. It was the army which dictated everything. It was the army which threw down governments, which dismissed governors, which put certain politicians on a black list, which insisted on the choice of officials, which excluded officers who did not obey the secret orders.

There were three problems in Spain which became well nigh insoluble. After the catastrophe of July, 1921, in Morocco, Spain could neither withdraw from this fatal region nor pacify the territory which she had undertaken to pacify. The responsibility for disaster was to be found in high places.

The second problem was that of Syndicalism—that is to say, of a somewhat violent form of trade-unionism. The centre of this movement was at Barcelona, where the working classes were prepared to revolt. The government of Barcelona was given to generals who instituted a reign of terror. Bands of assassins operated with impunity. Politicians were disposed of in the most ruthless manner. Agitators were swept out of the way.

The third problem which was treated with equal lack of intelligence was that of the Nationalist movement in Catalonia. It was after a long spell of Conservatism that the so-called Liberals again took office. It was generally felt that there should be a complete renovation, for Spain had fallen from the point of view of government as low as it well could fall. Militarism, one would have thought, was for ever discredited by the disgraceful mismanagement which had been clearly demonstrated in Morocco. But the Liberals showed the utmost weakness. Had they relied upon the people they might have succeeded. But as soon as the bishops pronounced against secular reforms, all idea of religious liberty vanished. As soon as the government attempted to proceed against a rotten militarism, generals protested with menaces and the government became impotent.

It was in these conditions that the government of Primo de Rivera was born. It was a return to the *ancien régime*. It was not a revolution; it was the reaction. The generals who were responsible for the repression in Barcelona were given power again. The constitution was virtually abolished. The liberty of the press and of public meetings, relative as it was, disappeared. A sort of permanent state of war was instituted. The regionalist movement in Catalonia was broken up without mercy, and the language and literature of the country forbidden.

The exile of de Unamuno is only the symbol which happens to have struck the imagination of the world of the intolerance of the Spanish *directoire*, which has reverted to the worst traditions of Spain.

Sooner or later, even in Spain it will be found that action and reaction are equal and opposite; that repression and revolt are equal and opposite. Any consideration of the person of Primo de Rivera must induce an indictment of militarism, which makes not for strength but for weakness. Militarism may be a weapon which it is useful to employ in certain circumstances; but militarism as a power can only be a dangerous thing for itself and for the country in which it flourishes. If Spain is infected with militarism, it does not follow that Spain is militarily powerful. It is the precise contrary that is true. Although the Spanish army is more costly than that of any other European country in proportion to the resources of the country, the army is helpless and hopeless, and Spain is almost without defence.

One of the most eminent Spanish politicians has pointed out that Spain has had to support 20,000 officers and a headquarters staff suf-

ficiently large to have commanded the entire
armies of Germany.   If ever Spain were attacked, she would succumb almost without a
blow.   Yet the civic strength of a noble people
is sapped to maintain what is called the prestige
of this mock army.   Something like a military
trade-union was organised and the army became
not only autonomous but the real authority.
Spain is ruined for the sake of an army which
could not with modern instruments of war overcome the rebellion of a handful of Moors without
effective weapons.   It is the army which has
stood in the way of progress; it is the army
which has destroyed liberty; it is the army
which has made of Spain the byword of
Europe.

And yet Spain has, in spite of reason, in spite
of experience, remained proud of her army.
While everything else was decaying, it was felt
that the army upheld the old traditions.   It
stood for pride, for courage and for patriotism.
The paradox that the repository of Liberalism
was the army is, of course, nonsense.   If the
army conspired and delivered *pronunciamientos*,
it merely manifested its lack of discipline.

I have said that there are three great Spanish

problems—but in a certain sense there is only one: that of the army. No words could be too strong to denounce this institution, whose baneful effects are surely apparent to all eyes. The army for years has ruled Spain, and if a rude shock was administered to the military spirit by the defeat of Melilla, if for a moment the Juntas were officially dissolved, the occasion was quickly seized to reinforce the power of the army and to make it more than ever the master of Spain.

The Cortes has long counted for nothing. The army has long counted for everything. What will be the end, it is hard to say, but it is reasonable to suppose that Primo de Rivera is the last card of the reaction.

I cannot conclude this short sketch of the Spanish Dictator and of the conditions which made him possible without emphasising the intellectual and artistic tendencies which have manifested themselves in the twentieth century in Spain. The political disorders, the economic difficulties, the attempted repressions, have not crushed the spiritual forces but have rather given them a new impetus.

At the head of the writers, philosophers,

artists, is Miguel de Unamuno, who may be taken to be the antithesis of Primo de Rivera. In literature, Benito Perez Galdas was followed by Palacio Valdès, Vicente Blasco. Ibanez cannot be omitted, nor can Pio Baroja. Among the younger men is the extremely original Ramon Gomez de la Serna. In painting, Picasso has influenced the whole of European art. In music one finds such names as those of Albeniz, Granados and Manuel de Falla.

In the theatre there has been a magnificent renaissance. In science, despite ecclesiastical discouragement, great strides have been taken. In short, the future of Spain must not be judged by political events; must not be judged by the emergence of Primo de Rivera; but must rather be estimated in the light of this wonderful efflorescence which gives the promise of even greater things to come. Spain, which is one of the oldest countries of Europe, which has contributed much to the world, in architecture, in art, and in literature, including the incomparable Cervantes with one of the five greatest books which have ever been written, has yet much more to contribute to the world.

But it will be in spite of, not because of, the

army, the church, and the throne; not because of, but in spite of, Primo de Rivera, that Spain will still stand gloriously triumphant in the annals of mankind that are yet to be written.

VIII

THE hopes not only of the Radical Party but of the Socialists in France have centred upon M. Joseph Caillaux. Internationalists of all colours abroad have also looked to M. Caillaux as their leader. Probably against his desire, contrary to his will, the most miscellaneous collection of idealists and mischief-makers has ranged itself in the party of M. Caillaux.

Of all the men I have known, M. Caillaux has one remarkable quality developed to an incredible degree—that of serving as the magnet to which fly foolish thinkers and sincere men of good will, and the most disreputable and sinister kind of person who moves in the diplomatic field.

It is more than possible that M. Caillaux is merely unfortunate in the company which has imposed itself upon him. He is an extremely able and I believe perfectly upright man. But wherever he has gone, whatever he has done, there has been lurking around him in the shadows an unavowable gang. Even some of the best members of the Radical group about him have had unfortunate experiences which their adversaries did not hesitate to recall from time to time.

This newspaper editor has committed an indelicate action in his college days. That other prominent person has been mixed up in a political scandal. They may be perfectly innocent or, at any rate, be guilty of nothing more than indiscretions, but somehow a strange odour clings about an extraordinarily large proportion of the friends of M. Caillaux. Napoleon believed in a star which carried him from victory to victory. Caillaux certainly has some baneful star which leads him into quagmire after quagmire. There are, indeed, some men iike that— men who cannot touch anything without it turning out badly.

The legend which has grown up about M. Caillaux is that of a great financier who alone is capable of saving his country from bankruptcy and ruin. To this legend is added the belief that he alone can make peace with Germany. It would be difficult to justify either statement. Certainly M. Caillaux is not to be despised as a financier. On one point he was supremely right. He introduced the income tax as it is known in England and now in America, into France. Although the system of direct taxation is somewhat foreign to French traditions, and aroused much opposition, and continues to arouse much opposition, it is clear that France could not afford to leave untapped such a source of revenue.

It will take many years before the income tax is accepted fully and is collected efficiently, but progress is being made. It is to M. Caillaux that the credit for taking an unpopular but necessary step must go. But it will be remarked that many of his misfortunes have flown from this act which made deadly enemies for him in France.

The income tax seemed to be regarded as a kind of Socialism. It was regarded as the despoiling of the rich. Even now the French do not understand the justice of the income tax when impartially applied. They are prejudiced against it, and it will be many years before their education will be complete in this matter.

There was a rather stupid cry at one time of "equality of taxation." Everybody should be "equal before the *impôt*." It sounds plausible enough, but when analysed it means that rich and poor are to pay alike to the State. Since taxation is to be levied upon articles and not upon persons, and since the taxed articles include the necessaries of life, it is not unfair to say that there would be, under such a system, not much difference between the contributions of the rich and the contributions of the poor.

Now that M. Caillaux should have helped to give the deathblow to this doctrine is excellent. It is his principal claim to be remembered. In defence of the French dislike of the income tax, it should perhaps be pointed out that the Frenchman does not admit anybody into his confidence about his private affairs, especially about his business affairs. He thinks he has a right to conceal his income, even from his own family. In other countries, a man's income is known to his neighbours and he is ranked according to our snobbish notions which judge of the value of a man in accordance with his wealth.

His income is known because he lves in such and
such a kind of house, and lives i such and such
a manner. He has been taugh to keep up appearances; that is to say, to rake the most of
his means, to indulge in outward show. He is
hurt if he supposes himsef to be considered
poorer than he actually is.

Now, this kind of snobbery, which enables a
man to accept the income tax, is almost unknown
in France. The Frenchman feels no compulsion
to live in a certain style. He lives as he pleases.
In the same house of flats there may be the greatest possible differences in the financial situation
of the occupants, but they may be socially equal.
Poverty is not a crime in France as it is in Anglo-
Saxon countries. Riches are not necessarily the
passport to society. A man is taken for what he
is and not for what he has. If one is to understand the French dislike of the income tax, one
has to bear in mind this traditional reluctance
to discuss money matters with anybody. To
be compelled to fill up papers declaring one's
exact financial situation is felt to be a great
hardship. That the State should have the right
to inquire into a man's means of living is felt
to be inquisitorial.

M. Caillaux ad to break down these preju-
dices. He had tɔforce upon the French a system
of taxation, agaist which their whole instincts
and practices cried out. While it is impossible
not to approve of his income tax policy, which
proved to be an essential reform for France,
where government finance has always been
inadequate, M. Caillaux did not show much
tact; he did not sufficiently take into consideration the deep-rooted objections of his compatriots. But tact has never been the shining
virtue of M. Caillaux. On the contrary, he is
a headstrong, authoritative man. Making a
superficial appeal to democracy, he is, in reality,
the true type of autocrat. He could not bear
contradiction; he grew furious if he were opposed.
M. Caillaux is a man of immense pride; he has
an overweening conceit of himself. One used
to watch him in the Chamber, his head thrown
back haughtily, his bald skull growing purple
with throbbing blood-vessels, whenever anyone
ventured to differ from M. Caillaux.

It is his stiffness, his irascibility, his intolerance
of others, his contempt for the intelligence of
others, his belief in himself as an altogether
superior person, which has made of M. Caillaux,

in spite of his one clear-sighted political act, a failure complete and undisputable in politics. He practised the ungentle art of making enemies better than any man I have known.

Now, although M. Caillaux was an inspector of finances and in Parliament was the advocate of the income tax, and has since the war written some fairly sound—but by no means unimpeachable—articles and books on reparations and the general financial situation, I have sought in vain for conclusive evidence that he is a heavenborn financial genius, who more than any other Frenchman, indeed, alone of Frenchmen, can restore order in French finances. This legend is pure nonsense.

One could name at least half a dozen men whose ideas are sounder, and who at the same time possess personal qualities of statesmanship that are totally lacking in M. Joseph Caillaux. His return to active public life could only arouse violent opposition and would set Frenchmen by the ears. One can understand his partisans in France clamouring for him; but that observers in America and in England should argue that peace and prosperity will come only with the return of M. Caillaux is to me incomprehensible, for if there is one man whose return will mean strife and division that man is M. Caillaux.

His supposed indispensability in the making of peace with Germany is equally a fiction. Precisely because he has always been suspected and accused of pro-German sentiments, he is the last of all Frenchmen to be entrusted with this delicate task. Any arrangements which it were possible for M. Caillaux to make would be resented in France as a humiliation, as an unpatriotic concession. It is a Nationalist, not one who is held by many of his compatriots to be an anti-Nationalist, who alone is capable of bringing about a reconciliation, if genuine reconciliation between France and Germany is indeed possible. For M. Caillaux to attempt a *rapprochement* with Germany would inevitably create a dangerous uproar; not only would he fail to promote peace between France and Germany, but he would create a greater antagonism than ever on the part of many Frenchmen towards Germany, and he would provoke beyond doubt a perilous conflict in France. There would be a reaction which would make matters infinitely worse.

I am not writing this out of any personal feel-

ing against M. Caillaux. On the contrary, I
have the utmost sympathy for him and consider that he has been placed in a false and unfortunate position. He has become one of the
martyrs of French policy. He has suffered
undeservedly as few men have suffered He has
been persecuted for his opinions and I am always
with the persecuted. But it has become necessary to destroy entirely erroneous suppositions
that have sprung up, not so much in France itself
as in America and in England, regarding the
personality of M. Caillaux and his possible
influence on events. His influence on events
can, after all that has happened, only be bad.
The evil fate which has pursued him will not
cease its pursuit, and the wisest course that
M. Caillaux could take for himself, for his
country, and for the world, would be quietly to
retire from active political life, or, at any rate,
confine his energies to the writing of books and
of articles, of fashioning policies which others
may apply.

Frenchmen will never forget that was
M. Caillaux who at the time of the menace of
Agadir, in 1911, surrendered a portion the
French Congo to Germany. They will never

forgive　m for this. It is possible to argue that
this w　an act of wisdom; it is also possible to
argue 　t it was an act of folly. In this con-
trover　 it is better not to take sides. There is
so mu　 to be said both for and against. It
may 　 that M. Caillaux staved off war. It
may 　 that M. Caillaux made war more certain. 　is opponents declare roundly that Germany not a country to be bought off, and that
the 　akness which France displayed in the
nego　tions of that day merely encouraged
Ger　ny to suppose that France would be an
easy　ey.

T　 suggest that if France had stood up
firm Germany would have understood that
it w　not by bullying, not by war-like methods,
tha　e should proceed. However this may be
fro　he German point of view, what is clear is
that 　 Agadir incident aroused such passion
in F　ae that M. Caillaux was thrown down
and 　Poincaré was put in his place. M.
Poinc　has, in one way or another, more than
any o　 Frenchman, dominated the international　uation ever since. So that even those
who 　pt the view that M. Poincaré is the
evil g　s of Europe, and should be put on the

same plane as the German Kaiser, must cknow-
ledge that M. Poincaré was given his opprtunity
by the diplomacy of M. Caillaux, il that
therefore M. Caillaux is ultimately repnsible,
whatever were his intentions, for what; since
occurred. Needless to say, I do nc iccept
such a view of M. Poincaré, but simpl sek to
show that even the best that the friens if M.
Caillaux can say for him, still leaves le jues-
tion whether his dealings with Germar id a
good or bad result quite open. Thre was
additional bitterness owing to the fit that
M. Caillaux negotiated with Germany rei the
head of the Foreign Minister in his Cint—
M. Justin de Selves. This was condeled as
improper conduct.

The prejudice which has thus acculaed
against M. Caillaux was intensified whei litle
time before the war M. Calmette, the cor of
The Figaro, published a number of imite
letters written by M. Caillaux and signe 'Ton
Jo" in which politics were discussed confidially.
These letters were of a compromising chcter.
They might have been sufficient to havriven
M. Caillaux out of public life. But wc was
to happen. Madame Caillaux, a revr in

her mu called on M. Calmette and shot him
dead in is office. It is true that a Paris jury,
after t fashion of Paris juries, acquitted her
of mur. The deed was done because of the
strong motions which had been naturally
arous in Madame Caillaux by the publication
of the intimate letters.

Ne theless, the political position of M.
Caill had surely become hopeless, even
thou Madame Caillaux was acquitted. It is
diffi to conceive the husband of a woman
who d killed a man in order to protect the
repu ion of her husband becoming Prime
Min r of a country where he would again be in
the of the whole world.

I even more. Rightly or wrongly, during
the r M. Caillaux was arrested on a charge
of gerous and unpatriotic conduct. After
re ing for two years in prison, M. Caillaux
was ndemned by the Senate sitting as a High
Co of Justice. The major charges against
hi were dismissed. Nothing definite was
in proved against him. He should certainly
ha had the benefit of the doubt and should
n ave been deprived of his political rights.
T was much that was arbitrary, both in the

launching of the charges, his imprisonment and the decision of the High Court. But accepting, as one does, the innocence of M. Caillaux, the evidence against him was still troubling. There seemed to have gathered about his person a whole host of adventurers, intriguers, spies and traitors.

It is possible, as was urged during those long days when in the Senate I watched the trial of M. Caillaux, that if the lives of other French statesmen were examined as minutely as was the life of M. Caillaux, as many rogues and unpleasant persons could be found to have touched them at some point or other. This is, as I say, possible, but the fact remains that the one whose war career seems to have been shot through and through with mysterious, dark acquaintances, was M. Caillaux. His ill-luck was pursuing him still. Never in modern times has a politician been pursued so relentlessly, dogged at every footstep by an unhappy fate.

Even setting aside this hotchpotch of suspicions, what sticks above all is the project of a Dictatorship which M. Caillaux drew up and deposited in a strong box in a Florence bank. This paper was entitled "The Rubicon." The

title signified that if once the project received
the beginnings of execution, there could be no
turning back. Now, M. Caillaux properly in-
sists that as a statesman he was entitled to
place upon paper, intended for no eye but his
own, any ideas which happened to occur to
him.

His habit was to jot down his thoughts in
rough form. It did not in the least follow that
he accepted these passing fancies. It did not in
the least follow that they had any serious mean-
ing. It was not his fault if these papers were
brought to light. The answer is a good one.
There is a good explanation, indeed, of every
episode in the career of M. Caillaux. But,
surely, it must be admitted that it was impru-
dent to preserve such records of his secret
thoughts. And surely it must be admitted that
when once it was for any cause made public
that M. Caillaux was capable of thinking of
himself as dictator, he could hardly expect the
country to look upon him in future without
suspicion.

Never have misfortunes fallen so thick and
fast upon any first-rank statesman in any
country. Almost everything he has done has

gone wrong. Unpleasant incident follows unpleasant incident. Revelation succeeds revelation; and although each one can be explained
away, the cumulative effect is unmistakable.
All this is not the fault of M. Caillaux, who
cannot even permit himself the luxury of writing
notes for his own consideration or letters for
one pair of eyes, without their becoming public
property. But the man seems to be under an
evil spell. One can only look at him askance.
To me it is inconceivable that he could ever
again return to full power. The verdict against
him may be quashed; he may sit in Parliament;
he may be the leader of a Party. But as Prime
Minister, he would surely be the target of too
many indignant Frenchmen, who do not believe
that accident can follow accident, coincidence
be piled upon coincidence, without implying,
if not the entire temperamental guilt of M.
Caillaux, at least some Jonah-like quality, which
is best thrown overboard.

In the Radical Party itself new chiefs have
arisen who know not Joseph—who would be
exceedingly jealous were he to replace them.
One may look upon M. Caillaux as a political
tragedy; one may consider him to be the most

unfortunate of men, a genius thwarted by untoward circumstances; but that he can still emerge from the dark cloud is almost unthinkable.

IX

THE future of Mr. Lloyd George can hardly be foretold. In England there is a general break-up of the parties and nobody knows how things will shape themselves. Some day perhaps there will emerge a true centre party. If it does, undoubtedly Lloyd George will be its leader. In it there will be found such men as Lord Birkenhead, Mr. Winston Churchill, perhaps Mr. Austen Chamberlain, and even Sir Robert Horne.

The truth is that neither the Conservative Party nor the Liberal Party is anything more than a shadow of its former self. One of them is led by somewhat incompetent men and the other is in the doldrums, deserted by its rank and file.

Now Mr. Lloyd George is not the man to tolerate such a situation for long. He has for years had a leaning towards a centre party. He is, as a politician, the most remarkable equilibrist. He stands, like an acrobat, first on one hand and then on the other. While nominally a Liberal, he in reality led the Tory Party, for it was the Tory Party which was the chief constituent element of the Coalition Government. When the Coalition Government broke up, Mr. Lloyd George went back to the Liberal Party. But he sees that the Liberal Party is losing ground in England. It does not appear likely to come back for a generation, if it comes back at all. Mr. Lloyd George is not the man after his tremendous triumphs to spend the rest of his life in a practically extinct party, deprived of means of political action.

Moreover, he is not even the chief in the Liberal Party. Even the disappearance of Mr. Asquith would leave others, such as Lord Grey, or Sir John Simon, with better claims than the prodigal son, who came back to the fold after riotous living. It will, indeed, be a pity if no opportunity is found of utilising the undoubted political genius of Mr. Lloyd George. It is with all the greater pleasure and sincerity that I recognise the splendid qualities of Mr. Lloyd

George, because I was among his most vigorous critics in the British press.

During the peacemaking he took in an opportunist spirit the wrong path, but his instincts were sound. His vision was clear, and had he possessed a little more courage at the proper moment, nothing but praise could be given to him. Unfortunately, when he found the whole of the British Parliament ranged against his conceptions of peace, he lost heart and meekly took the easier course of accepting the prevalent views. He did not even, like the would-be candidate, declare to the committee of selection, "Them's my sentiments, and if you don't like 'em, I can change them." He simply denied his own opinions.

One finds it hard to forgive him for his display of political cleverness during the years which followed the war, when what the world wanted was a display of political courage. But, if he tried to steer around obstacles, he saw his goal clearer than his compatriots, and in so far as he felt that he could progress towards that goal, he tried to do so.

Mr. Lloyd George is a man of action. He believes in doing things. He does not believe in standing still or risking complete failure. Therefore, when he finds it impossible to act as he would wish, he nevertheless acts—as others would wish. It is this love of action, whether good, bad, or indifferent, which has made Lloyd George what he is. He would have been a bigger man had he thought less about the results. But, for better or for worse, such was the cast of his mind that he strove to keep power and to accomplish even those things which were not altogether desirable, provided he accomplished something.

In earlier days he was indeed the fighter. He was not afraid of taking the unpopular side. He proclaimed himself against the Boer War. It is recorded that after one of his speeches at Birmingham he was so seriously menaced by the mob that he had to escape by a back door dressed in clothes obligingly lent him by a policeman.

He was, remembering his humble origins—though he is not as he likes to think, a child of the people, he is essentially of the middle-classes—the enemy of the rich—until he became rich himself. He began his campaigns against the land dukes. He denounced the manufacturers who saw in protectionism an opportunity for acquiring greater gains. He was what was called a "little Englander" and a Free Trader, and he fulminated in the Limehouse manner against the Conservatives. But even then, honest and daring as he was in his convictions, he saw with uncanny insight that he was really on the winning side. It was not long before popularity succeeded unpopularity. He had pushed himself to the front rank of British politics. He had far more fire than anybody else had ever shown. He did not trouble overmuch about good taste. He attacked with astonishing vigour. His images were such as could be readily understood by the people. He was, although Mr. Asquith was the Liberal Prime Minister from 1906 onwards, the true leader of the Liberal Party.

For more than sixteen years he remained Minister, and during the final five years he was Prime Minister of England with the heaviest responsibilities that could fall upon any man. They were the years of the war and the years of peacemaking. It is not surprising that towards the end of this long period of service he appeared to lose his grip and to become far less interested in his task. No man can go on forever. And swiftly and completely Mr. Lloyd George not only ceased to be Prime Minister, he ceased to be a commanding figure in British public life.

He was plunged into obscurity again. His followers were scattered. Nobody troubled particularly what Mr. Lloyd George said or wrote or thought. It is amazing that a statesman who has had almost despotic power, who has enjoyed a personal rulership rarely equalled in British history, should sink to the lowest depths of public indifference. It happened almost overnight; but the truth is, of course, that for a long time the prestige of Mr. Lloyd George had been sapped and he only awaited the blow which would bring him down.

The same fate happened to him as he had prepared for Mr. Asquith. During the war a little conspiracy suddenly overthrew his chief and placed Mr. Lloyd George at Downing Street. It was perhaps time; for that indescribable thing which we call "grip" had been lost by Mr. Asquith and it was impossible to allow him to continue in office when the issues were so grave, when the issues were the existence or destruction of the British Empire.

I do not think it is a proper charge against Mr. Lloyd George that he did not remain faithful to Mr. Asquith. Personal loyalties are excellent, but loyalty to the country, loyalty to the public good, cannot be subordinated to personal loyalties. As Prime Minister, Mr. Lloyd George more than justified the methods which his friends had adopted to elevate him to the supreme post. He was a dynamic force as Mr. Asquith could never have been and it was his dynamic force which helped to win the war.

At the Peace Conference in Paris, when his power and prestige were at their height, he might have proved to be a much greater man than he showed himself to be. Had he made a firm stand, it is possible that he would have rallied the whole feeling of England in favour of a peace which would leave no gaping wounds in Europe. Instead of taking the wiser course, he became the mere demagogue. He went to an election on the cry of "Hang the Kaiser" and the cry of "Germany will pay." He thus tied his hands. Nobody took the threat to hang the Kaiser very seriously, but the promise to make Germany pay to the uttermost farthing was taken seriously by almost everybody.

Impossible conditions were demanded by the French. Although they had for fifty years smarted under the loss of Alsace-Lorraine, they wished to reverse the position by detaching Rhineland from Germany. They declared that the frontier of Germany should henceforth be the Rhine, and although they disclaimed the idea of annexation, something indistinguishable from annexation was among their demands. In the end a compromise was reached by which Allied troops were to remain in Rhineland for fifteen years and a clause was inserted in the Treaty under which the French claim they are empowered to prolong indefinitely the occupation of this German territory in the event of the nonfulfilment of all the Treaty obligations and in the event of their being unsatisfied with the guarantees for their security. This measure was bound to engender bitter feelings. It is no wonder that Germany sought to evade the payment of even just reparations. But, indeed, impossible reparation burdens were placed upon Germany, as we have come to see.

Now against all that in his opinion was unfair in the draft Treaty, Mr. Lloyd George undoubtedly protested. He drew up a memorandum which Signor Nitti afterwards published in his book on the peacemaking. This memorandum corresponded to an interview which Mr. Lloyd George had given me about the same time and which I published in *The Westminster Gazette*, then under the editorship of that great journalist, Mr. J. A. Spender. He pleaded for moderation. All who spoke with him at the time are aware that he foresaw all the difficulties which have since accumulated. They are aware that he deplored a Clemenceau peace, realising that if the Treaty were not to be a healing Treaty, it could only be the charter of future wars.

For my part, I am certain that had he boldly told the truth he would have been listened to. There was a real desire among men for a true peace. But, unfortunately, when he was asked to explain by hundreds of Members of Parliament who sent a message to him in Paris, he went back to London and repudiated the sentiments which are to be found both in the interview and in the memorandum.

Lately he has made the charge that it was during his absence in London that President Wilson and M. Clemenceau arrived at an agreement behind his back. Technically, it is true that during his absence there was an agreement, but he immediately subscribed to it and he subscribed because he had committed himself once more to a fatal course in the British Parliament.

There are many things in the Treaty, or which inevitably flowed from the Treaty, that are to be deprecated. Such was the occupation of German territory; such was the arrangement about the Sarre. Such, too, was the subsequent division of Upper Silesia. Such, above all, were the exorbitant demands for reparations. Mr. Lloyd George cannot escape his share of blame for all that has happened to Europe since 1919. But one has no desire to press this point. The whole world was mistaken and it is too much to expect that one man should have stood out. All that one can say is that had he and President Wilson been more in accord, had they united their forces, there was a chance that something better would have been achieved. Europe was plunged into the terrible and protracted dispute about reparations.

The tactics of Mr. Lloyd George had much to commend them. He was conscious that the economic possibilities had been surpassed, and he tried desperately hard to bring France to accept his point of view. But France became suspicious of him. When he denounced Germany the French did not believe him to be sincere. When France agreed to the reduction of her claims she believed that Mr. Lloyd George was hostile to her. She saw that the British had got rid of the German fleet which was the chief menace to England. They saw that England had obtained possession of German Colonies. They saw, in fact, that England had taken all that could readily be taken and had left France with hypothetical credits which grew more and more difficult of collection.

Mr. Lloyd George was, indeed, somewhat too astute in his dealings with M. Millerand and later with M. Briand. He seemed to get the better of them. He seemed to obtain to a certain extent his own way. In the end the French thought that it was Mr. Lloyd George who was helping Germany to evade her obligations, and who was whittling away bit by bit the just claims of France. Then it was that France, fearing that she was merely being towed in the wake of England, was becoming a second-rate power, called for a man who would stand up to Mr. Lloyd George and would say No.

At Cannes, Mr. Lloyd George appeared to be on the point of obtaining his greatest triumph of reaching a reasonable settlement with France and Germany. But at the moment of triumph, the French President and the French Parliament revolted. There was a terrible reaction. M. Poincaré became Prime Minister. With M. Poincaré, even Mr. Lloyd George could do nothing, for M. Poincaré simply dug his heels into the ground and refused to budge an inch. He declined to take part in any more spectacular Conferences. At the Genoa Conference, which had already been fixed in principle and could hardly be called off, M. Poincaré refused to go in person. He sent M. Barthou to represent him, with instructions that he should take no decision without first referring the question to Paris.

The distrust of Mr. Lloyd George on the Continent had reached its highest pitch. The legend had grown up about him that he could outwit and out-manœuvre French diplomatists with his magic tongue and his winning ways. "Therefore," said M. Poincaré, "I will not put myself in the path of temptation, but will remain quietly at home, will consider in the quietude of

the Quai d'Orsay any propositions which are
made, and will send my answer through M.
Barthou."

The Genoa Conference was a gallant attempt
to come to terms with Russia. But in the
prevailing conditions it was doomed to failure.
When it failed, Mr. Lloyd George's reputation
was shattered. He remained in office for some
little time, but he had been broken on the rock
of M. Poincaré.

The muddle could not have been worse; but
Mr. Lloyd George must be judged rather by
what he endeavoured to do than by what he
actually did. One cannot help thinking that less
noisy demonstrations, more private conversations, would have been more effectively persuasive. But Mr. Lloyd George had accepted the
generally accepted description of himself as the
"Welsh wizard." He had come to think that with
his genuine ability and his exceptional agility
he could overcome all opposition. He might
have avoided many difficulties had he not felt
that he could easily get out of difficulties when
they had once been created.

Now the difference between the supreme billiard player and the poorer billiard player lies,

I am told, in this, that the poorer billiard player is always bringing off brilliant shots, while the supreme billiard player rarely leaves himself a hard shot on the table. Mr. Lloyd George was always leaving himself hard shots and some of them were undoubtedly unnecessary.

He had, however, grown tired and such hero worship as was showered upon him is good for no man. In the British Parliament he was something more than a Prime Minister. Mr. Bonar Law was, in effect, his Prime Minister, and he was a sort of President. It was Mr. Bonar Law who led the House: Mr. Lloyd George had barely to put in an appearance.

In the old days it was said of Mr. Lloyd George by those who worked with him that he could neither read nor write. This is a malicious epigram, and had a certain truth: Mr. Lloyd George was neglectful and relied upon his unprecedented powers of improvisation, to prepare a case at the last moment, to get out of any trouble, to make a swift appeal which always succeeded. He succeeded too easily and he became less and less inclined to work. In the end, it was Mr. Bonar Law who broke up the Coalition of Conservatives and Liberals under Mr. Lloyd George, restored the independence of his party, left Mr. Lloyd George stranded and reigned for a brief period in his stead.

The Conservative Party, in its turn, quickly came to grief owing to the blunders of Mr. Bonar Law's successor, Mr. Baldwin. It lost its majority at a perfectly uncalled-for election. The Labour Party, although in a minority, was put in office by the Liberals. But the Liberal Party, which had been utterly smashed by Mr. Lloyd George when he formed the Coalition Ministry during the war, was in even worse case. It had never recovered and does not seem likely to recover.

Nothing was more surprising than the fact that the Liberal Party readmitted Mr. Lloyd George to its ranks when he was left without a party. The animosity between Mr. Asquith and Mr. Lloyd George had spread to the respective followers of the two leaders. The National Liberals—as the Lloyd Georgians were called—had taken almost the same hue as the Conservatives. The Liberals proper had taken down Mr. Lloyd George's portrait in the club which served them as headquarters and relegated it to the

cellar. Nothing could have reunited the two
wings except the defence of Free Trade, and
Mr. Baldwin had imprudently put forward
protectionist measures in the elections.

But Mr. Lloyd George is uneasy in the Liberal
Party, and the Liberal Party is by no means
enthusiastic about Mr. Lloyd George. Therefore, there are, as there were bound to be, fresh
signs of a new break-up of the Liberal Party.
Mr. Lloyd George still cherishes the hope that
a new Coalition can be made, a centre party,
which will absorb the more moderate elements
of the Liberal Party and the more moderate
elements of the Conservative Party. What
place, indeed, is there for a Liberal Party in a
country where there has been for many generations the two-party system, now that the Labour
Party has become a real power? Some of the
Liberals are drifting towards Labour; some of
them are drifting towards Conservatism. If
the process were to continue, there would
again be a two-party system in England. But
Mr. Lloyd George would be at home neither in
the Labour Party nor in the Conservative Party.
He would be at home nowhere but in a centre
party, which would embrace those Liberals who

feel that they can become neither Labourites nor Conservatives, and those Conservatives who feel that the mere negation for which their party stands is no longer practicable in the new stir and urge of things.

The future of Mr. Lloyd George will, therefore, be most interesting to watch for it may involve the future of England.

X

ANATOLE FRANCE, who is perhaps the most universally honoured writer in the world, this year passed his eightieth birthday. In the evening of his days he has continued to give us volumes of his exquisite prose, in which he looks back pleasantly on his earlier years, and in the setting sun remembers the dawn.

It is not only politicians who influence the course of events. Indeed, they are often but the fly on the chariot wheel. Rather is it the thinker, the writer, whose intervention in the world's affairs, though less conspicuous, less noticed, really helps to turn the wheels.

There are many resemblances between Anatole France and Voltaire. It was Voltaire's irony which was the most important thing in the eighteenth century in France. The Revolution was made by others, but the spirit of the Revolution was largely created by Voltaire.

Anatole France, whose wit, though not so
nimble as that of Voltaire, more melancholy
than that of Voltaire, has delighted not only his
own countrymen but readers in every country
for half a century, is not without his direct
action on affairs. His love of justice, his revolt
against vulgarity, mercantilism and Chauvin-
ism, has been expressed openly and boldly on
unpopular platforms. When the Communists
in France were being prosecuted, Anatole France
did not hesitate to write the noblest letters for
the most extreme organs on particular instances
of arbitrary exercise of power by the authorities.

He was not careful of his reputation, as he well
might have been. He did not consider that as
a man of letters he should stand aloof from the
controversies of his time, nor did he shrink from
incurring unpopularity, of turning his admirers
into enemies. His admirers, however, refused
to become enemies. When Anatole France
wrote something for which the common Socialist
had been condemned, his readers found either
that France was right, or that as an ageing man
he was not to be taken seriously.

But France had not waited until he was an
ageing man to utter his criticisms of the inequali-

ties of civilised society. Though never a fighting
man in the sense that Zola was a fighting man, although enveloping everything in a tender scepticism, a beauty of language which was rather
the honey of the bee than its sting, he yet
had never left his feelings for the under-dog,
his feelings against the mere exploiter or the
inhuman engineer of the government machinery,
in the slightest doubt. His social views can,
however, hardly be elevated into a philosophy.
France knows little of Marx or of the doctrines
of Lenin. Rather has he simply the cultured
man's vague dream of a better organisation of
society in which presumably everybody would
have leisure to cultivate the arts and surround
himself with grace and beauty.

Anything more opposed to the modern fever-
ish manner of living it would be hard to imagine.
There would be no jazz bands or dancing halls
or factories in which the machines are men and
men are the machines; no rulers who are at once
tyrannical and sycophantic before the mob; no
stock exchanges wherein to gamble with pieces
of paper which represent human happiness or
unhappiness—there would be nothing but pleasant pictures, admirably produced books, delicate

meats, and men and women not too passionate
but inclined rather to play with ideas and sentiments, in the republic of Anatole France.

All this is obviously not clear-cut enough to
leave any substantial impress on the time, but
the apostle of grace and charm, of intellectual
loveliness and melting melodies has, in spite of
appearances, left his traces in the hearts and
heads of innumerable men and women of our
age. The present phase will pass and the spirit
of Anatole France will yet come into its own.

The newer French writers are not at all of the
school of Anatole France. They disdain the
smoothness, the perfection of his style; they are
disjointed, incoherent, striving for brilliance and
cleverness at all costs. They have decided that
their generation is the generation of jazz and
their writings are exercises in jazz. Disciples
Anatole France certainly has, but they are not
the best known or the most typical French
writers. But that is of no importance. Fashions
come and fashions go, in books as in all else;
and long after the fashion of to-day has passed,
Anatole France will endure and be held as the
master of the years which bestraddled the
nineteenth and twentieth centuries.

In private life, Anatole France strikes one as the wise old man whom one may find in his books. He corresponds very closely to the conception which it seems to me one would have of him had one never seen a portrait, had one never met and conversed with him. It is probably the common pastime of most readers to draw imaginary pictures of authors, and seldom do those pictures resemble the reality. Writers are by no means like their books. Often one is disappointed to find the writer of grave and sagacious thoughts, squat and round and rubicund; or to find the creator of poetic fancies heavy and bearded; or to find the profound psychologist the perfect image of a prosperous business man. Nothing is more deceptive, nothing provokes greater illusions than the attempt to identify the writer with his works. They have often apparently no points in common.

But in the case of Anatole France, he has himself drawn his own portrait—if not of his physical appearance, at any rate, of his mental physiognomy—so often in his books that he is precisely what one would have expected him to be. He looks the erudite philosopher: calm,

composed, with just a trace of *tristesse* in the
general expression: with irony lurking about
the lips; with placid amusement peeping from the
eyes; with an indescribable air of goodness and
gentleness about him. He is fairly tall, with
long wrinkled brownish face, the strong nose
full of character, carefully trimmed beard, and
on his head a round red skull cap, which somehow hints of the eternal student. His movements are easy and almost nonchalant. There
is little passion but rather placidity and medita-
tive amusement with the spectacle of the world
which, hung in illimitable space amid the innumerable stars, is peopled by millions of little
scurrying, ant-like creatures, each of whom
supposes himself to be the centre and the *raison
d'être* of the universe.

In private life Anatole France is witty and
wise—though not so witty and wise as in his
books, for his books are the quintessential
France. He has never written easily. He has
always had to sift and strain and compose somewhat laboriously, to file his phrases to perfection. Nor does he invent freely. He confesses
that he *prend son bien où il se trouve*, that is to
say, that, like Shakespeare, like Molière, like

most of the great artists, he does not scruple to take the material which suits his purpose wherever he finds it, and work it in his own way. Curious stories are told of his methods of work. Indeed M. Brousson who was his secretary for many years has related how he makes use of the scissors and paste—that is to say how he often copies word by word from guide-books, histories, biographical dictionaries, a passage which he then works over again and again. Often he demands as many as seven successive proofs. His writing is painfully slow. An example of his way of transforming phrases may be given. From a biographical dictionary he copied this sentence: "The wife of Theroulde was rich and of good reputation." The sentence is flat enough but Anatole France waited until the proofs had been returned to him before re-writing the sentence as follows: "As the wife of Theroulde was rich, she was said to be of good reputation."

He throws upon the paper in the first place whatever comes fairly easily but he goes over his phrases again and again. Particularly does he in the process of correction seek to eliminate such words as "who" and "which" and "that,"

and to shorten every sentence. It is by patience
that he arrives at perfection.

If he is disillusioned about life, he still retains
a generous attitude towards life. He still,
though without self-deception, hopes that something finer will some day be fashioned, that
civilisation will be improved for all its children.
There is nothing fanatical in his conceptions:
everything is governed by perfect taste. Anatole France may be described as the highest
flower of culture yet produced, the topmost
peak of human intelligence. Culture is nothing
if it is not critical. Anatole France is essentially
critical, but even where he condemns, he condemns indulgently; and though he finds flaws,
he accepts with a remarkable eclecticism. If
he mocks the world, if he is sceptical of nature
and disappointed with mankind, he remains
débonnaire, and rarely allows himself to lapse
into indignation.

To what purpose? Indignant or complacent,
the world must be taken as it is and men as
they are. All one can do is to place oneself on
the heights, to survey all with the merest shade
of regret, though not of resignation; to enjoy
what is good and strive, not too hopefully but

nevertheless not too hopelessly, to change that which is evil.

Anatole France is indeed a superb critic. Sometimes I am tempted to regret that, large as the body of his work in literary criticism has been, he did not apply himself still more unreservedly, for a still longer period, to this particular task, in which I think he excels. Even such men as Sainte-Beuve are often cautious, often wrong. They are too timid; they accept the established values and are afraid of committing themselves to new judgments.

In the literary essays of Anatole France there is an urbane but incisive quality, a complete confidence, an absolute fearlessness. He is capable of liking the most dissimilar things while recognising their faults. He is never doctrinaire—he is too big to confine himself within the limits of preconceived opinions. He has no need of the foot-rule of readymade standards. But then is not practically the whole work of Anatole France critical? Is he not in all he writes, exercising his judgment, not in the manner of one who has made up his mind on literature, on politics, on life, and measures carefully everything in accordance with the precepts which he carries in a tool-bag by his side; but in the manner of one who brings a fresh, a living and an alert mind to every subject which he touches?

About the period in which Anatole France was born, that is to say, about the eighteen forties, there were also born many great French artists. One may mention—though the list is not exhaustive—Mallarné, Rodin, Verlaine, Monet, Cézanne and Pierre Loti. André Suarès has drawn an interesting comparison between Loti and France—France as the refined Parisian, whose outlook was however universal: Loti as the world wanderer, who was yet anchored, with all his exoticism, to his native land. There is much truth in the epigram.

France always remained in the sunny Tuileries, in the shadow of Notre Dame. His wanderings were among the book shops which line the quays of the Seine. But with the local colour of Old Paris infusing everything he wrote, his spirit traversed frontiers, traversed space. Local colour is, after all, superficial, and one may discover as much of the world and of mankind within sight of the Sainte Chapelle as in the remote temples and teashops of the Far East.

It was in a library that Anatole France was born, and he has haunted libraries ever since. His love of books appears in all his books, and what exquisite uses he makes of them. A library was his cradle and a library has always been his refuge—but not a refuge in the sense that he has sought to escape entirely from life. He has looked out of the library windows on large horizons. If there is a touch of pessimism, if he has felt the vanity of existence, he has remembered that literature is at once a part of life, and a reflection of life, in which the outlines are somewhat softened.

In his house in the Villa Saïd and at La Béchellerie, near Tours, there are not only beautiful books which it is a joy merely to handle, but a splendid collection of pictures, including Prud'hons, which perhaps help us to realise his wistful, deliberate romanticism, which never forgets that it is romanticism, which never permits itself to be mistaken for the reality.

If Anatole France is conscious of the folly and even futility of things as they are; if he permits himself to indulge in raillery, he is never bitter but always smilingly ironical, and always does he seek to cast the soft glow of the imagination over all that he sees with his clear eyes.

Like Voltaire, he is aware of the imbecility of life, and extracts endless amusement, though a somewhat pathetic amusement, from the raree-show. But much more than Voltaire, he is also aware of the heroism of humanity and the aspirations of humanity. His treatment of young artists has always been extraordinarily courteous and generous. He does not allow himself to be deceived but he does not allow the fear of deception to dry up the wells of kindness.

It has been objected that although the style of Anatole France is absolutely pure, it is perhaps too artificial; it shows too much learning; there is too much play of erudition; too consciously a juggling with ancient ideas found in ancient books and pleasantly analysed in the crucible of modern science. There may be some justice in this criticism. But the manner of Anatole France is the inevitable result of a critical attitude towards life, a critical attitude which detects all the weak places, all the botched construction; but which tenderly, gracefully, while revealing the errors, enwraps them all in an artificial illumination of supreme goodness.

Anatole France may be a pessimist, but he is a pessimist who helps towards a better appreciation of the possibilities. He is a pessimist as was Omar Khayyam when he wrote:

Ah Love! could thou and I with Fate conspire
To grasp this sorry Scheme of Things entire,
    Would we not shatter it to bits—and then
Re-mould it nearer to the Heart's Desire!

In a world which is changing, which sometimes seems to be in chaos, Anatole France is not, as is often pretended, the nihilist. He is the critic, and the critic is helpful. In his irony one constantly catches glimpses of beauty. By showing us life as it is, though without bitterness, he indicates life as it should be. He teaches tolerance and placidity in an age in which even the reformers add to the confusion by their reckless energy.

XI

EVEN in France it is found difficult to understand a man like Mussolini. When Signor Mussolini takes Napoleonic attitudes; when he wears laurel leaves round his head; when he is photographed with his pet lion; and when he comports himself generally in the most theatrical fashion, even the French, who are also of the Latin race, cannot refrain from laughter. They have an acute sense of the comic, and they find much in the recent history of Italy that is truly comic.

There could be no greater contrast between M. Poincaré, who never poses, and Signor Mussolini who poses all the time. In Anglo-Saxon countries it is still more difficult to understand the postures of the Prime Minister, or rather, the Dictator of Italy. But Signor Mussolini should nevertheless be taken seriously.

He is by no means a mountebank whom an accident has placed in power. Until the elections this year, it might have been doubted whether his power reposed upon a solid foundation. But since those elections it has become clear that he represents his country and is likely to do so for some time to come. He has struck precisely the right keynote for the Italians. He incarnates their idea of the new Italy which is an Italy of energy. It was for lack of energy that Italy was beginning to decay. Then came a magnificent revival which manifested itself in the arts as in politics. Even d'Annunzio, whose literature was languorous and decadent, preached the gospel of energy and practised it, too. It was from Italy that various ultra-modernist movements in painting and in writing came. It was in Italy that was born the energetic method in politics which is known as Fascism.

There is much to criticise, there is much that one can only deprecate in Fascism, but there is little doubt that Fascism saved Italy. That, surely, must be counted to its credit, and whatever the means and whatever the character of the men, the end was worth while. It was not so much Bolshevism in the Russian sense with which Italy was menaced, as mere degeneration. Nobody who travelled in Italy during the years which followed the war could fail to be struck with the apathy with which the country saw itself crumbling to ruin.

There was a breaking-up of institutions, a lack of patriotism, a violent conflict of classes, economic disorganisation and financial chaos. The mass of the people had become lethargic. The moral of the nation had sunk to the lowest ebb. The successive governments were quite unable to cope with the anarchy which was rampant. It was in these conditions that Communism made rapid progress. The authorities, from the King downwards, remained inert, dismayed, and did nothing whatever to stop the rot.

Whatever one may think of Fascism, however one may disapprove theoretically of the conduct of its adherents, it can hardly be denied that Benito Mussolini arose at the right time to pull together his country. What has been called the Crusade of the Black Shirts began. The Fascists took vows of discipline and devotion to their country. Their sober uniform was a stroke of genius; it had the true transpontine touch; it commanded respect. They deliberately marked themselves out when it was dangerous to be marked out. Danger has always had an attraction for men, and nothing could have ensured the rapid growth of the organisation more than its appeal to the love of adventure, as well as to the love of certain simple but eternal ideas.

And, indeed, the Fascists, fanatically as they behaved, really were in peril. They suffered for their cause; violence was certainly not on one side. The country looked on with growing interest; the lackadaisical mood began to disappear. The people were thrilled by this spirited fight, of the Fascists against the Bolsheviks. Something like one hundred and twenty armed men, many of them like Mussolini himself, ex-Socialists and ex-Syndicalists, at last marched on Rome, determined to obtain power, to scatter the effete Ministers, to rally the Italian people.

There was much that appeared like play-acting in Fascism, but there was also a real purpose, a sincere belief. Mussolini was the inspirer and the captain. There could be no resistance when he and his men marched through the streets of Rome for seven hours, an army of black shirts and tasselled caps, carrying carbines and triangular flags. They were acclaimed by the populace; they were saluted by the King. One must forgive much to men in whom faith burned, who, in spite of showy gestures, had adopted self-sacrifice as a creed, had adopted patriotism as a religion.

Sir Percival Phillips, in his excellent though rather onesided little book on the history of Fascism, has quoted a typical oath of one of the local bands of Fascists. It reads: "By the blood of our two thousand martyrs whom we invoke as witnesses and judges of our action, we the Black Shirts of Piaceza swear that for one year we will not wear on our persons any gold, silver or other precious metals or stones. We will work ardently without pay for the good of our country. We will give all superfluous ornaments to a fund for supporting enterprises having goodness, civilisation, beauty and civic improvement as their objects."

Now one can be exceedingly critical of many of the superficial manifestations of the Fascists, but one cannot condemn those who took such oaths and who in fact put them into practice. Italy was stirred. Workers asked to be allowed to work overtime for the State without extra pay. A sort of voluntary taxation was imposed upon themselves by many thousands of Italians. Anti-patriotic organisations were swept away. Communism was ruthlessly suppressed. Indiscipline, which was rampant in the army and in the workshops, was changed to willing obedience. Agitation of all kinds, the seizing of factories by the workers, the seizing of lands by the peasants, ceased.

It is strange to reflect that Mussolini, the son of a blacksmith who was a Socialist, and who was himself a Socialist, who had indeed fled from his own country and who had been banished from other countries, such as Switzerland, was the man who struck the blow at a particularly noxious and degenerate kind of Socialism.

The breach between Mussolini and the Socialists came with the great war. He put patriotism first and Socialism second. His paper, the *Popolo d'Italia* though nominally Socialist, urged Italy to act. It was not, however, until after the war when Italy was ill-governed and was heading straight to disaster, that Fascism was born.

At first the movement did not grow quickly, but the seizure by d'Annunzio of the disputed port of Fiume gave a direction and a patriotic

purpose to the Fascist organisation that helped
it considerably. Then followed a long period of
illegal action. The Fascists were attacked and
they attacked in their turn. Street fights became common. But the chief weapon of the
Fascists was castor oil which gangs of Mussolinists administered to Socialists and Communists wherever they were to be found.

The authorities, who had been helpless against
Communism were equally helpless against Fascism. In 1921 the Fascists were an organised
military force which was to be found in every
district of Italy. They responded to orders with
remarkable obedience, and growing bolder and
bolder, at last went out on expeditions, occupying
towns that were in the hands of the Communists. They showed the utmost resourceful-
ness, and although the whole story of their
exploits has never yet been adequately told,
many of the incidents which have been recorded
prove that extraordinary courage, amazing discipline, and a supreme directing intelligence,
were exhibited throughout the whole period of
the formation and the development of the Fascist organisation.

Although Mussolini had republican leanings,

he decided that it would be better to preserve the monarchical traditions of Italy, and when the final struggle with the government towards the end of 1921 came, the King wisely put himself on the side of Mussolini, and Mussolini put himself on the side of the King.

It is, however, in the use of his power as Dictator that Mussolini should be judged. Parliament submitted to him, and there can be little doubt that his rule has been efficient. He has restored Italy to something of her old greatness. The country is at work; it is taking its proper place in the Councils of the Nations. Its economic situation is still precarious but it has been improved in a manner that seemed impossible to all of us who knew the Italy of a few years ago.

Mussolini has shown himself to be ruthless towards incompetent officials. He has demanded real services, and he has obtained them. The spirit of the people has altogether changed. Until this year Mussolini governed as it were with a whipped and cowed parliament. He governed because he possessed his own private forces. He had to impose himself on parliament and on the people. Now his position has be-

come more constitutional. Two-thirds of the
Chamber, after the elections, are Mussolinists.
With such a majority, he can at last declare
that his government rests, not on force, but on
the consent of all classes of the nation.

It is now for him, if he is wise, to work for
appeasement; to restore liberty; to return to
normal and legal methods. It remains to be
seen whether such is his intention. For it cannot be denied that while the administration of
Mussolini was perhaps excusably arbitrary during the early days, it would be lamentable were
he to continue to commit or to permit outrages
on freedom, which would quickly make his
administration scandalous and dangerous and
would, in the end, bring it to the dust.

Mussolini has shown that he has claims to
greatness. He was great because he availed
himself of an opportunity for service without
counting the cost. No mere ambition could have
carried him to the topmost pinnacle of power.
Histrionics or no histrionics, Mussolini must
have felt deeply or he could not have acted so
perilously and so energetically. He abolished
factional quarrels which were bringing Italy to
naught. He swept away a corrupt and inefficient

bureaucracy. He gave leadership when leader-ship was badly needed.

Against most of his principles, if indeed he has any stable principles, one could say much. But one cannot refuse to admit that historically Mussolini was needed, and that his tactics, however disputable in themselves, justified themselves by their success. One cannot therefore refuse to regard him as a great man; for great-ness, after all, chiefly consists in taking oppor-tunities. There is no such thing as luck and accident in political life. Or rather, the timid man, the short-sighted man, the man who is not a born leader of men, fails to take his chances.

But the question remains, now that Mussolini has formally established himself on the will of the people, can he show true statesmanship? There are signs that after the storm and stress of the past few years, Mussolini is genuinely settling down into a constructive statesman. He has noisily fulminated against little States; he has stood up boastfully to bigger powers; but he has nevertheless, in spite of outward appear-ances, in spite of theatrical poses which appeal to the Italian temperament, really striven to keep the peace.

In foreign affairs his great achievement, as I see it, is the renewal of good relations between Italy and Yugo-Slavia. Although his Ruhr policy has been ambiguous and displayed rather too much Machiavellian prudence, it was, on the whole, right. He has undoubtedly made Italy a strong, industrious, disciplined and peaceful nation.

But it is now time to revise his methods. He cannot, unless he wishes to provoke a reaction, continue to treat his adversaries illegally. He must learn, as one writer put it, "where dictatorship ends and vulgar tyranny begins." Bands of armed Fascists still terrorise men who are guilty of nothing more than an honest expression of views; men who do not overstep the limit of fair political criticism. Mussolini cannot be held personally responsible for the many incidents which have occurred, but no government which is to last can build itself upon the doctrine of violence.

Much has been written during the past few years of the barbarous behaviour of the Bolsheviks. If Italy under Mussolini is to continue to employ violence against the critics of the government, it is difficult to regard it as essentially different from Russia. Ideas of democracy and of liberty are in the long run a necessity for a modern state. The complaint of Mussolini against previous Italian governments was that they did not suppress ruffianism; they did not really govern. Mussolini has now to decide whether he is going to suppress ruffianism, whether he is going to govern according to the precepts of civilisation. It is hard perhaps to hold his followers, who have helped to place him in his position of supremacy, in check, now that their work is accomplished. But such a decision he must take, and the Fascists themselves must endeavour to conform to law and order. If he takes the opposite course; if bands of Fascists are still to behave irresponsibly and arbitrarily, terrorising and bludgeoning their adversaries; then it is certain that they will in the end destroy Mussolini, as every despot has been destroyed.

He has his parliamentary majority; he has his constitutional position. It is on the recognised forces of law and order that Mussolini must rely. If he relies upon bands of personal followers, he will provoke a revolt. His dictatorship of violence must be transformed into a moral dictatorship. One cannot ask too much. One must give Mussolini, who has undoubtedly achieved wonderful things, some breathing space. But ultimately the measure of his greatness will be decided, not by how long he can maintain himself as Dictator, but how long he requires to transform himself into an ordinary Prime Minister, governing, not by fear, not by armed bands, but by the will of the people, by the principles of democracy.

XII

POINCARÉ: THE UNROMANTIC BOURGEOIS

NOTHING has puzzled the on-looker more than the immense influence of Monsieur Poincaré during a long period of years. For this influence, although supreme in his country, was obtained without the smallest appeal for popularity. Indeed, I have rarely known a statesman who was, in some respects, more unpopular than the former President of the French Republic.

Sometimes in the early days of his premiership, when his avowed policy was to coerce Germany, one went to the cinemas of Paris where the doings of public men are recorded week by week. One went because it is in the cinemas in France that one can best appreciate the sentiments of the people. They clap or they hiss in frank undisguised fashion whenever popular or unpopular personages appear upon the screen. Now when M. Poincaré appeared they did not applaud. They were cold and suspicious, when they were not, as in some of the more crowded districts, really hostile. I saw this manifestation of public apathy too often to suppose that it was accidental or indigenous to one particular quarter. Somehow the name of Poincaré had become connected in the French mind with the war and with the disappointments of peace. Somehow there was a fear that he would lead his country into fresh adventures that might end disastrously. In any case, there was no warmth, no cordiality, no enthusiasm, for the man who has more than any other statesman dominated France for a generation.

But this does not mean that M. Poincaré was not accepted, that he did not represent the people, that France could, as it were, be divided into two parts—one part containing M. Poincaré and a few hundred deputies and the other part containing the rest of the French population. Such a conception has only to be stated to reveal itself as grotesque. The enigma of M. Poincaré was precisely this: that he did represent adequately and faithfully and more than any other man the new France, which had forgotten the humiliation of defeat in 1870, which had shaken off the supposed attempt by England to fasten a diplomatic yoke upon her, but that he never seemed to be taken to the heart of France as was, for example, M. Clemenceau.

Far more than M. Clemenceau could ever represent France—except in glowing episodical moments—Poincaré has embodied the new spirit of a France which had determined not to quail, not to be subservient, to stand erect and proud and smiling. The reason for this extraordinary authority, combined with lack of popularity is, however, not far to seek. M. Poincaré is essentially the unromantic bourgeois. He has nothing of the flamboyancy of Clemenceau. He shrinks from melodrama. He genuinely endeavours to efface his own personality. He does not try to be splendidly eloquent, like M. Briand, and he does not provoke admiration by his resourceful cleverness. He is studiously plain, straightforward, precise, with a rigidity that has given false ideas of his character. He was never supple, because he detested that adroitness which has marked some of his compatriots in passing off concessions as triumphs, in reversing policy and pretending to have scored.

This is only another method of describing M. Poincaré as scrupulously honest in word and in deed. Honest he is, and it is because he is honest that he is respected, but respected without fervour. Foreign politicians who happened to have based their success on their adroitness, were dismayed to find M. Poincaré so unyielding. They abused him, as perhaps no European statesman has ever been abused abroad, because he would not play the game, because he would not help them to perform their conjuring tricks, or perform conjuring tricks himself. M. Poincaré it seemed was not of their kind. Now opinions may still differ about M. Poincaré, but history will record that whatever he was or was not, he was honest—the honest bourgeois.

Most of the epithets which were showered upon him really mean the same thing. When he was described as narrow-minded, when he was described as obstinate, he was in fact being described as honest. Dexterity he detested. Juggling with phrases he abhorred. He expressed himself in downright fashion and he stood by his phrases because they were for him the exact political truth. In the long run one must, even though exasperated by such obduracy, admire the man who takes no theatrical poses, who relies upon no fine gestures, who does not seek to get out of his own commitments. One knows where one is with Poincaré, and the phenomenon of a man who had made up his own mind, who knew his own mind and who would not deviate from his principles, was so novel in the post-war Europe that few people could understand and few people were not bitterly angry with it. They thought that if they grew angry enough, if they directed the batteries of their denunciation upon him for long enough, M. Poincaré would furtively produce a little white flag in one hand, while still waving the French tri-colour with the other hand.

This is the whole explanation of the unprecedented attacks that were made upon him by foreign countries. It is the whole explanation of how the French themselves, tired of mere trickery, tired of the *panache* which politicians and poets alike affect in France, gave their fate into the keeping of M. Poincaré as they had given it into no other hands for fifty years, while still remaining lukewarm towards the man who never flattered them and was never demagogic. Has not M. Poincaré himself given the clue to his character in declaring, "Popularity and unpopularity mean nothing to me. I shall go on doing what I conceive to be my duty, whether people like me or dislike me."

Never did M. Poincaré seek the limelight, although the limelight has beaten upon him as upon few men. His predecessors in the post of Prime Minister, and the Prime Ministers of every country, loved the display of the conferences which were held from time to time and with increasing frequency in all the capitals and casinos of Europe. An army of reporters went from town to town, writing indefatigably about the peacemakers as they had written indefatigably about M. Clemenceau during the war. Very little was accomplished; the resolutions taken at these conferences were both useless and contradictory.

Men who had taken up a certain attitude in 1919 took up the opposite attitude in 1920. They were amazed that M. Poincaré, then neither President of the Republic nor Prime Minister of France, should stand in the background proclaiming the rights of France, proclaiming respect of treaties, and proclaiming the necessity for consistency. He went on pro-

claiming these things with a pertinacity that
impressed the French people. There were
many who were annoyed, who regarded M.
Poincaré as a spoilsport, a marplot. But in the
end, after all the play-acting, there was no
option but to give effective power to M. Poincaré. His sincerity was perceived by the French
people. They were uneasy about this sincerity.
They were not sure that he had taken the best
course. They would have preferred a little more
complacency; they would have liked to give up
the struggle.

They regarded M. Poincaré with some misgiving, even while they felt that they had to
give him their confidence. Here was a man
who would never let them down; a man who
would never deceive them. It is perhaps a mistake to suppose that the unromantic bourgeois
is rare in France. The world has grown accustomed to the more showy type of Frenchman.
There are, indeed, plenty of showy Frenchmen,
but the solid qualities of France are based upon
the unromantic bourgeois.

Nor should one suppose that this plainness is
a synonym for commonplace mental attain-
ments. M. Poincaré is one of the most gifted

men of his time. He has succeeded, not merely
as the politician, but as the lawyer, and as the
writer. Before he definitely plunged into the
political arena, he had made an independent
fortune at the bar. He had placed himself above
the temptations which beset the politician in
France. The *assiette au beurre* is a phrase which
is freely used in France. It corresponds to
"graft." And, indeed, politics for many men
furnishes not only a career but a living. For
M. Poincaré it did not furnish a living; it fur-
nished only a career. He built his career upon
his financial independence.

Among the wild charges which were hurled at
Poincaré when it was the custom to abuse him,
was a suggestion that he was in some way in the
pocket of the   mité des Forges. It was an
altogether unworthy suggestion. When he was
a lawyer, M. Poincaré appeared in commercial
cases and worked for large companies; but that
he has ever put himself under any obligation to
the large companies is a palpable libel. Everybody who knows M. Poincaré knows that in this
respect also he has always been honest.

Again, in the interval of his Presidency and
his Premiership he returned to journalism. He

became perhaps the most powerful journalist that France has ever produced. His power resided in his sincerity; that is to say in his mental honesty. He was incorruptible, not only in the vulgar sense that he was inaccessible to monetary considerations, but that nothing, certainly not the promise of popularity or of prestige, would induce him to palter with his thought. He wrote without circumlocution exactly what he believed and nothing else.

The world may regard the Ruhr experiment as a mistake, but the world should at least regard the Ruhr experiment as the mistake of an honest man. When M. Poincaré consented to take office after the fall of M. Briand, he could have had only one object—to serve his country. He had been President of the Republic for seven years, the seven most terrible years of modern French history. Surely, this was enough for any man. None of his predecessors in that office had ever dreamt of returning to the political arena to become an active politician dependent on parliamentary votes, liable to suffer the humiliation of defeat. They had retired on their laurels when they were allowed to retire—that is to say, when the cares of their office had not killed them, as they had killed more than one President.

He might well have thought that he had done enough for his country in guiding it through the vicissitudes of the war. What possessed him, after occupying the highest post to descend to a reputedly lower platform, where he would be the target of all men, from which he would be sooner or later in all probability ignominiously cast down? What possessed him was and could only be an ardent patriotism. He could not stand aside and see reparations, which had been promised, whittled down; he could not stand aside and see his country cheated by Germany and deserted by her Allies—worse than deserted, subjugated to their will.

Not only was it clear that Germany meant to evade her obligations and that the Allies of France were inclined to favour Germany in this design, but it was also clear that Germany was preparing her revenge and that, sooner or later, unless something were done, France would again be invaded. It was further clear that the successive capitulations of French Prime Ministers had not won the gratitude of those coumtries which had demanded such capitulations, but were merely the starting-point for fresh demands and were losing for France the place which she had occupied and deserved to occupy in the world's affairs.

France was, in fact, descending to the rank of a second-rate nation. It was, in the opinion of M. Poincaré and of all patriotic Frenchmen, time to react against this laxity. His methods may have been wrong but his all-compelling purpose was undoubtedly right. Weary of the heavy weight of administration, he might proper-ly have followed the example of all his predeces-sors, and like M. Fallières, have gone to trim his vines. He had done his part; nothing could hurt him more. His place was marked out in the history of France. If a new war came the responsibility would not be his. In his country retreat, he would be untouched.

That he did not heed these prudential con-siderations is, whatever may be thought of his policy, surely to his credit. He heard the call to throw himself again into the fight for his country and he heeded it. Personal comfort and safety would have dictated another course. The battle in which he engaged was one which he was just as likely to lose as to win. It re-

quired the highest courage for him to take the
decision which he took.

M. Poincaré possesses the highest courage,
but it is not that comparatively simple courage
of the full-blooded fighting man. On the contrary, M. Poincaré is excessively timid by nature. He shrinks from action. He counts the
cost. Clemenceau during the war went into the
front line trenches in his hale, hearty manner,
slapped the soldiers on the back and spoke
cheery words to them. M. Poincaré also visited
the battlefields, but he made no impression on
the soldiers, because he did not possess that robust
physical courage which M. Clemenceau had.

One will never understand M. Poincaré unless
one realises that essentially he is timorous. But
it is precisely the timorous man who is capable
of the highest nervous exaltation, who, knowing
his duty, conscious of the possible personal consequences, will somehow or other see things
through. This is, as I have said, the highest
kind of courage, and M. Poincaré required every
ounce of this courage to accomplish what he has
accomplished for France. There were moments
when the whole world stood aghast, when the
whole world denounced M. Poincaré. But,

tremblingly perhaps, wrestling with himself, M. Poincaré stood firm and would have suffered any kind of martyrdom rather than yield. Perhaps he was more unyielding than he would have been had more conciliatory methods been used towards him. But you cannot shift this particular type of timid courageous man by menaces. He will stand firm against all bullying; he will remain at his post while he is being torn in pieces, and if the heavens fell, he would allow himself to be crushed under the ruins.

Unfortunately, this kind of courage is not widely understood and the statesmen of other countries who opposed M. Poincaré were utterly blind to its existence in M. Poincaré.

Above all, M. Poincaré is nothing if he is not a worker. He is the most gigantic worker I have ever known. He does not work in great bursts of energy; he remains steadily at his desk from morning till night, month after month, year after year. His prodigious industry is rendered possible by the Spartan simplicity of his habits. He can hardly be persuaded to make use of mechanical aids. His state papers and his correspondence, even of the most insignificant kind, he conducts himself. He perhaps wastes himself in detail, but he nevertheless keeps his essential purpose before him and is not to be deflected. He seems to live for nothing but work, and if for no other reason, one should have the highest veneration for a man who spares himself not at all.

Of his limitations it would be possible to say much. He is somewhat lacking in humour; he is almost too earnest. His imagination is small though his memory is prodigious. His speeches, which he first wrote and immediately memorised, are monotonous in their insistence. A little more readiness to readjust his position, to bring it into consonance with that of others, would often have been an advantage. But we all have the defects of our qualities, and the particular qualities of M. Poincaré would not have been intensified to such a degree had he not renounced the cultivation of other qualities.

This is not the place to analyse his policy and its results. But whatever view is taken of his work, it cannot be denied that he has sacrificed everything to his intense patriotism, and that the man, as distinct from his policy, is a man of whom France may well be proud and to whom history may well render justice.

XIII

D'ANNUNZIO: PRINCE, POET, POLITICIAN

A POET made a prince: does not that inspire us with hopes that the artist is at last coming into his own? But, after all, there is no such departure from the traditions. If Gabriele d' Annunzio has been created a prince, it is not because he is a great writer, but because he, too, has been the patriotic politician. It is not because of his magnificent if languorous prose that he is honoured, but because of his intensely active life. It was when Italy celebrated the anniversary of the Fiume settlement that the author of the raid on Fiume was given the title of Prince of the Snowy Mountain.

Gabriele d'Annunzio, in his retreat at Cargnaceo, above Gardone-Riviera, on the Lake of Garda, may often have had bitter thoughts about the Italian authorities who, after all, drove him from Fiume when he had seized it for his country. But the authorities have repaired this fault: they have recognised that D'Annunzio made it possible for them to obtain their present control over the Adriatic port.

It was over this town that the Peace Conference in Paris in 1919 nearly came to grief. President Wilson declared that he would return to America: he issued a manifesto over the head of the Italian representative who was claiming Fiume. He brought upon himself the splendid thunders of D'Annunzio who, in enchantingly fantastic and exaggerated language, denounced the Wilsonian teeth, the British breakfast, and American habits, all in the same sentence. Then, not content with mere words, he went off and seized Fiume—a gallant modern adventurer with the fine swashbuckling spirit of another age. Politically, one could only hold up horrified hands: morally, D'Annunzio's exploit was to be deplored. But anybody with the sense of a story, anybody who loves personal daring and picturesque valour, could not but admire the heroic writer who could put colour into his life as into his books.

Be it remembered that Mussolini had not at that moment been invented. The Prince of the

Snowy Mountain must often regret that he did not persist in his course, and instead of in the end surrendering Fiume into the hands of a properly constituted government, make himself Dictator, not only of Fiume but of the whole of Italy. For undoubtedly D'Annunzio missed his opportunity. He might have been the Mussolini of Italy. He might have been the saviour of his country. He might have wielded supreme power instead of living, as he now does, in dignified retirement. It is true that he is a prince, but he is a prince in exile, when he might have been a reigning prince. Still, he has his compensations. He has missed the Dictatorship but he is nevertheless regarded as the most glorious of Italian figures, and he is treated royally. Around him is a retinue. He has his household—nay, his court, in the beautiful property of Cargnaceo, and delegations visit him with a great stir and pother, producing the impression that this quiet spot is somehow the centre of great bustling State affairs.

It is D'Annunzio who, when Unamuno is expelled from Spain, crushes the Spanish Directoire with his scorn in resounding messages which are flashed round the globe. It is D'An-

nunzio who, when la Duse dies in America, sends
to Mussolini a request, which has the air of a
command, to bring back her body for State
burial in Italian soil.

If he does not wield material power, he is still
the true moral force in Italy and his pronounce-
ments in his grandiloquent style have the effect
of ukases. He is, as it were, lifted above the
world, but from his Olympus directs the world.
It is, after all, a great life for he can not only
play his practical part, but may still cultivate
his soul, may still write his beautiful books, may
still worship the sun.

How different—and yet how similar—is his
present life to that which he lived before the
war in his self-imposed exile in France! For the
life of Gabriele d'Annunzio, in spite of its brilliant show, is still an internal drama, as it was
then. He cherishes his ideals of magnificence
and power now, as he did then. And if to-day
the external appearances of things better corre-
spond to his own conceptions, that is more or
less accidental and relatively unimportant. Under the pine trees by the sea in France, as he
paced restlessly with his gambolling dogs, he cast
himself for the rôle of principal actor in his own

epic. Never could he compress his energies within the covers of a book. Those who knew him then, knew that his ardent spirit was not of the *litterateur* who weaves around himself a web of words, or, if the web were woven, it was woven only to give him a chrysalis shroud from which he should soar, a winged hero in the storm and sunshine over a heaving world.

There is an amazing contrast at first sight between the slow-moving rhythms of his artistic productions and the swift flashing rhythms of his actual life. But if one considers more carefully, one will see that if as a writer his greatest preoccupation has always been to make his personages move in accordance with the laws of music, and to place themselves in a series of pictorial or statuesque attitudes, precisely the laws which govern these personages have governed D'Annunzio himself. Every gesture might be seized by the sculptor. His carefully prepared scenes are fit subjects for the painter. He ascends and descends the scale of emotions with the dexterity of the supreme musical genius. Now it would be altogether wrong to regard him as a vulgar and insincere actor. The impulse is a genuine artistic impulse, which has long been trained to

produce itself in rhythmic perfection. **Perhaps**
nobody in our day has the same sense of the
drama of attitudes. But just as his plays are
all attitude, and one grows weary at last of the
long-drawn-out posturings in *Le Martyre de
Saint Sébastien*, so one may grow a little weary
of the perpetual posturings of D'Annunzio.

When first the conviction that he was reserved for a great destiny grew in his brain, he
might as well have wondered what glorious
career could await him in a humdrum age.
Europe was at peace. There seemed to be no
scope for an adventurous spirit. But the Man
awaited the Hour, asking himself when the hour
would come and in what shape, but ready to
tingle into more terrible life than any of his own
passionate creations. Whatever volcanic forces
were in the people of his imagination were in
him, slumbering uneasily and demanding their
release. His lyricism was but a prelude, a
preparation for the greater lyricism of his life.
Symbolist, he sought a new kind of art, an art
which should be a synthesis of all the arts. In
his life he sought a new kind of intenser living
in an intenser world. But how could he achieve
his purpose? The poet would seem to have no

place in politics, no place in action. A situation which is theatrically impeccable might have the most disastrous results in reality. Æsthetically, we may applaud Nero and regard it as a sublime tragedy that Rome should flame for him like a torch. But, practically, we cannot afford to burn down Romes to provide the appropriate stage setting for a poet-prince. However much D'Annunzio and his friends may suppose themselves to have had a political purpose, the truth is that he has had a purely poetic purpose in all that he has done, as in all that he has written.

It was in a serene sky that the world war flamed forth and suddenly D'Annunzio realised, not that he was Italian, but that he was Italy. Henceforth he personified his country in all her fierce beauty and pride. Italy thought that she thought: but she only felt. D'Annunzio entered upon the scene of the war with unfailing instinct at the exact moment, and in that unique hour he stood uniquely for Italy.

Who that was in France or in Italy during the war days does not remember the wild excitement that greeted D'Annunzio as he darted to and fro. One forgot the physical incongruity of this middle-aged man as he wielded his sword-like eloquence. He was transfigured by a wild joy. There was nothing feigned in his fervour. An immense ecstasy possessed him. The burning words which enflamed his compatriots were spontaneous. They gushed from him as lava gushes from Vesuvius. But somehow he remained a conscious Vesuvius, a Vesuvius directing every spark.

He took to aviation, finding a new zest, an unknown romance, in flying above battlefields and mountains. His triumphs in the air quickly made him a legendary hero. Above the clouds was he not more than mortal? Those were great days, those days of the great war; and tragic as they were for most of us, they were for D'Annunzio an inextinguishable joy.

After the war, what remained for him, now that he had tasted such sublime tragedy? Would not the world become flat, stale and unprofitable? Would not the remaining years be an anti-climax? But, no. Peace also has her triumphs no less renowned than those of war. The fight for Fiume had begun, and the dream of a League of Nations was, thanks to D'Annunzio, in danger of being drowned at the bottom of the Adriatic.

With a few thousand men he took possession of the town and threatened to take the Dalmatian towns. Everything was pitched in the heroic key. If one regards the matter in cold blood, it may appear that he did not help Italy or humanity. What was wanted was not a buccaneering expedition, not a crusade of nationalism, but peace and protection from revolution and friendship among nations. But D'Annunzio could not, being what he is, do other than give rein to his poetic instincts. He could not realise that these sword and cape adventures, these grandiloquent speeches, had for background a dark confused curtain, and had for auditorium a howling theatre.

Italy had broken with the Entente. America was shocked. There was little aid forthcoming for a distressed country where the black bread of war was still being eaten, and where meat and coal and other necessaries of life were not to be obtained. There were the wildest Socialist movements. However fine the play was for D'Annunzio, Italy might well have perished in the threatened chaos. To win Fiume and to lose all the rest was politically unsound.

New European wars might easily have broken

out. The House of Savoy might have collapsed
and the destruction of Italy have been accomplished. The King of Italy and the Italian
Government scarcely dared to protest, although
they had before them the catastrophic downfall
of dynasties—the Dynasty of the Romanovs,
the Dynasty of the Hapsburgs, the Dynasty of
the Hohenzollerns, and all the princely families
which had fallen from the Rhine to the Vistula.
But D'Annunzio was not deterred by the menace
of a distressed and angry proletariat. He was
inspired by poetic insanity which had abandoned
all pretence to prudence. He scattered with
incoherent prodigality his splendid words and
fulfilled with heedless *outrance* his romantic
rôle.

Everybody will rejoice that Italy has been
saved from the grave disorders in which at that
time she might have been engulfed. It is perhaps well that it was Mussolini and not d'Annunzio who came forward to accomplish the
larger task; for, with all his great qualities,
D'Annunzio was not the man to take in hand
the situation which had developed. It could be
urged that Mussolini is also theatrical. But
with all his *beaux gestes*, Mussolini possesses a

great deal of sound statesmanship. His flourishes are, as it were, extraneous ornaments.
They may help him in his popular appeal; but
the basis of his success is his capacity for solid
work, and the underlying cautiousness of his
policy. With D'Annunzio all prudential considerations are cast to the wind. He is moved
only by his sense of drama. Therefore, although
superficially there is a good deal of resemblance
between Mussolini and D'Annunzio, fundamen-
tally there is the greatest possible difference in
their temperaments.

If D'Annunzio still thinks of himself as a
possible rival to Mussolini for the favours of
the patriot party, he is mistaken. He could not
have performed the task that Mussolini has
performed. In spite of outward appearances,
D'Annunzio's policy would have been destruc-
tive, while Mussolini's policy is constructive.

Doubtless D'Annunzio helped to revive patriotism in Italy by his narrowly nationalist
appeals; but the use he would have made of the
patriotic revival would almost certainly have
been disastrous; whereas Mussolini, appealing
to the same sentiments, using ostensibly similar
methods, has, one may hope, really welded the

new Italy and has brought about a revival in which the whole world rejoices.

It is better that the parts have been allotted as they are. D'Annunzio is and must be "the infant of volupty" the irresponsible poet, the mad dreamer, the lover of sensation, of magnificence, of spectacle, of drama. It is better that while Mussolini governs, D'Annunzio should remain a popular but a retired hero in his charming Cargnaceo property, receiving his guests, pleased with the comings and goings, playing at politics; but also writing his *Notturno*.

The house in which he lives was owned before the war by the daughter of Richard Wagner and her husband, Thode the historian. It was sequestrated when Italy declared war on Germany and was bought from the government by D'Annunzio. It is a two-storied white frescoed building, with green shutters. Over the door is the inscription "Clausura Silentium." Terraces go down to the lake, with cypress, oak and laurel trees in the grounds. On a little hill there is a monument to Victory. On certain anniversaries D'Annunzio lights commemorative fires. The snowy Alps stand sentinel.

There let us leave him, among his symbolical

columns, this strange, ardent, poetic man; who has had perhaps greater moments than anyone now alive, and who has had an excessive sensibility with which to taste their full savour, and who, moreover, has left to posterity, not merely records such as the politician leaves, but emotions permanently imprisoned in monumental language.

XIV

SIR WILLIAM GOODE: THE SAVIOUR OF NATIONS

SIR WILLIAM GOODE may not be as well known as many less important people but he may truly be described as the saviour of nations.

He has saved Austria; he is now engaged in saving Hungary. What the peacemakers of Paris set out to destroy, he has set out to restore. More than any one man in Europe, he has nursed back sick peoples iu life and health. He is the physician who is called in when the case has become desperate. He may yet be called in to take a hand in the saving of Germany.

Every American, English, Italian, French journalist, every newspaper editor throughout Central Europe, every Minister on the Continent, knows Sir William Goode. His popularity is extraordinary. It is more than respect that one feels for him, even if one should happen to be a Czecho-Slovakian or a Rumanian., He has had at times to work against the statesmen of the Little Entente, who in some respects at first were inclined to short-sighted policies. But although they regarded Sir William Goode as their greatest diplomatic opponent, they always displayed the utmost courtesy towards him, and, indeed, professed and felt personal friendship. Well they might. It is impossible not to like the good-humoured, breezy Newfoundlander who, in spite of his joviality, is as shrewd as it is possible to be and never misses a point of the game.

He had to fight every inch of the way when he went out to make a virtual end of reparations in Central Europe. He recognised at an early date, as a handful of impartial observers recognised, that whatever might be said for or against the whole theory of reparations as applied to Germany, the attempted enforcement of reparations in Central Europe could only mean ruin and chaos. Neither Austria nor Hungary were in a position to pay reparations after they had been left reduced to mere shadows of their former selves. Austria was once a great and proud nation, forming with Hungary an immense Empire. Suddenly it was cut down to a tiny tract of territory with a large city, Vienna, as its capital. Austria resembled a tadpole with a huge head and no body. The inhabitants of Vienna, to whom a great country had paid tribute, found themselves obliged, so to speak, to take in each other's washing in order to obtain a living. The tiny circumscribed Austrian State could not support a capital like Vienna. All around were hostile States.

Austria would have been glad to have joined up with Germany but the Treaty forbade such an amalgamation and France flatly asserted that she would never allow the junction to be effected. Austria seemed doomed to decay and a painful death. The Austrian money depreciated with lightning rapidity. Administration became impossible. The Viennese were the helpless victims of the decisions of Paris. They lost all heart. What could they do to defend their interests? What hope could there be of escaping the doom which had been prepared for them—the dreadful doom of starvation! Since they could not produce for themselves, and since they had no money to buy abroad, their extinction seemed certain. Vienna simply sat silent waiting for the end.

The case of Hungary was not quite so bad but it was bad enough. The Magyars are a more spirited people than the Germans of Austria. They resisted better. The conditions, it is true, were not so hard for them. They could at least produce the necessaries of life. But, on the other hand, the most dreadful events happened in Hungary. There was a Red rising and a White reaction. When Bela Khun attempted to make of Hungary a Soviet Republic on the Russian pattern, the world looked askance and hardened its heart against Hungary. When Bela Khun was swept away, and Admiral Horthy acted as Regent, Hungary was denounced everywhere as the home of the reaction in Central Europe. It was well known that Hungary, with its deep-rooted traditions, which Bolshevism had failed to pull up, wanted to become a kingdom again. Kingship in most countries in Europe has become synonymous with militarism. And, indeed, hand in hand with monarchism in Hungary went militarism. Rumania was afraid that Hungary would attack her. Czecho-Slovakia was on the alert. Hungary had become in Central Europe the enemy: she had no friends: she was isolated, although she kept the flag flying as gallantly as might be. Her money, too, began to depreciate. Hungary was going, though at a slower pace, the way of Austria.

The outlook was black enough, and it seemed almost impossible that Central Europe would ever settle down again. It was then that Sir William Goode stepped in and transformed, after some years of hard work, the whole situation. During these years I saw much of him, and in so far as I had opportunities of helping, gave him that support, in the old Westminster *Gazette*, the London *Times* and the *Christian Science Monitor*, and in other American and English publications, which was necessary if the bad feelings which had naturally been created by the propaganda of the Little Entente were to be calmed.

Sir William Goode has a remarkable career. He is an English subject but he has served in the United States cavalry, and for some years was an American newspaper reporter attached to the *Associated Press*. He has frequently told me of those early American days when he suffered the greatest hardships. When he enlisted in the American army he was without food. Perhaps these experiences gave him a better human understanding of the misery of Central Europe than the well-fed diplomatists, who think not in terms of humanity but in bloodless academic terms, could ever have. It is easy to cut up countries and to frame treaties if one leaves out of consideration the consequences to the peoples with whom one is dealing in a heartless superior manner. But Sir William Goode knew that there is a human side to international politics.

After serving on the staffs of New York papers and as special correspondent for the *Associated Press*, Sir William Goode gained a still wider experience of life as an English journalist. He was managing editor of the London *Standard* (famous in its day but now dead) and afterwards news editor of the *Daily Mail*. Northcliffe at that time was endeavouring to see the human side of diplomacy and Sir William Goode was an apt pupil. Northcliffe was a great man who has been much misunderstood and maligned by that school which still thinks that diplomacy should preserve the character of a mysterious profession. Its secrets should never be divulged to the public, accord-

ing to this little group, and they resent any
attempt to break down the close corporation.

Goode was again to realise that nations are
composed of individuals with necessities which
must be met, when he became liaison officer
between the British Ministry of Food and the
United States and Canadian Food Administra-
tions during the war. He was also Honorary
Secretary and Organiser of the National Committee of Relief in Belgium, working whole-
heartedly with Hoover. In these immense
activities of providing food for various peoples,
he was engaged until 1920, when he was made
President of the Austrian Section of the Reparations Committee.

It is now I think no secret—or at least it ought
not to be—that from the beginning Sir William
Goode made up his mind to torpedo the Austrian
Section of the Reparations Commission. He
saw that it could not work; that it was adding
insult to injury to demand from Austria, which
had been battered to pieces, relief for countries
which were much stronger. The peacemakers
were either ignorant or were indulging in the
most amazing irony when they proposed that
Austria should pay. Sir William Goode saw

more clearly. He realised that it was for the other countries to come to the assistance of Austria, not for Austria to go to their assistance.

I think it should be remarked, though money matters obviously cannot take more than an incidental place, that Sir William Goode was, as President of the Austrian Section, paid a very large salary which he could, had he practised the customary official hypocrisy, have continued to draw for a number of years without accomplishing any work except that of watching Austria drift from bad to worse. It is not perhaps to his special credit that he preferred to sacrifice his salary. One would like to suppose that anybody in his position would have done precisely the same thing. But, unfortunately, one knows that many people would not have done this thing. At any rate, the Austrian Section was, thanks to Sir William Goode, speedily wound up.

But this was not sufficient. Reparation demands were still being made upon Austria, and although the machinery of collection had been practically scrapped and the whole world knew that there could be nothing to collect, Austria nevertheless needed outside assistance. Sir

William Goode was asked to become financial adviser to the Austrian Government. He voluntarily threw himself into this new task. He went carefully into the accounts. He ably presented, little by little, the true case of Austria to the various governments. He carried on a discreet propaganda. Rarely did he come into the limelight himself. Never did he divulge a piece of news that had not its definite purpose to serve. He was helped by his old newspaper connections. He knew, as it were, how to handle the press. Every pressman was a colleague. Gradually the facts were understood, and in the end, as everybody knows, all the countries concerned agreed to relinquish their prior claims on Austrian assets and allow those assets to be used for the raising of a loan under a scheme prepared by the Financial Section of the League of Nations.

Austria has made good; Austria has shown that she was to be trusted. New heart and hope was given to the Austrian people who, after the initial financial assistance was forthcoming, began to work out their own salvation.

After Sir William Goode, the present Chancellor of Austria, Monsignor Seipel is the man who is most responsible for her remarkable recovery. It is strange to find a priest, who had never particularly concerned himself with politics, in the position of Chancellor. But he was emphatically the indispensable man. He is a man of exceptional intelligence and he is trusted. He is a Christian Socialist in the best sense of the term. For him, too, it was a sacrifice to devote himself to public work, for his health was precarious, and until he took office he was obliged constantly to absent himself for long periods. The odd thing is that since he has given himself up entirely to public work he has managed to forego his "cures" and instead of being any the worse, his health has improved.

In the background in Austria there is a strange figure of whom little is ever heard. He is a lawyer with the most acute brain. His financial knowledge is profound. He has become a confidant and adviser, a sort of *éminence grise*. Since he resents attention being drawn to him, I will merely state that this remarkable person seems to have come straight out of a weird story of H. G. Wells. He is a man with a tremendous head and with no legs.

When the salvation of Austria was assured,

Sir William Goode was asked to render similar services to Hungary. This was a harder task, for at least in the case of Austria everybody recognised that the country was harmless; whereas in the case of Hungary what most of the people in Central Europe saw was that she was dangerous. Undoubtedly Hungary is potentially dangerous, but all countries respond to kindly treatment. If Hungary is harassed and oppressed, the proud spirit of this people will find the way out in war. Hungary, unlike Austria, would not lie down and die. She would bring down with her in her fall those enemies who would exult in her fall. But if friendship is shown her, she will respond, as indeed, she is responding.

There is room for all the little nations that have sprung up in Central Europe on condition they do not shut themselves up in water-tight compartments, on condition that they do not regard their neighbours as their enemies. It was more difficult to convince the world of the pacific intentions of Hungary, and it was more difficult to arrange for a certain release of the liens held by the Reparations Commission on Hungarian assets, before the League of Nations could produce another loan scheme. But Sir William Goode, in the face of much opposition quietly, skilfully, pursued his purpose. Having helped to save Belgium, having helped to save Austria, he has now saved Hungary. What new task remains for him in a world in which there are more statesmen engaged in destruction than in construction?

The present Prime Minister of Hungary resembles the type of cultured English country gentleman more than any foreign statesman that I have met. He has exquisite manners, and although he can put on an impenetrable armour of dignity when he pleases, in general he is exceedingly amiable. It is seldom that one can honestly write of a politician that he, after only a few meetings, not only impresses one with his ability but endears himself by his gentleness. In talking with Count Bethlen, as with other Hungarians, it is exceedingly difficult to imagine that the Hungarians are a warlike people, only dreaming of aggression. They have a peculiar charm. The Finance Minister, Baron Koryani was, before his appointment, for some time Minister of Hungary in Paris, where he, in spite of the strained rela-

tions between Hungary and the Little Entente,
somehow contrived by his ingratiating manner,
which is however anything but sycophantic, to
develop friendly relations with the Ministers
of Yugo-Slavia and of other Central European
countries. If only suspicions could be put
aside, as they now doubtless will be, there
would certainly be no reason why the neighbours of Hungary should not live on terms of
amity with this essentially likable people.

A proverb of Benjamin Franklin has it that
"God helps them that help themselves." The
world might well help Hungary for it cannot
be insisted upon too much that Hungary has
helped herself. Without waiting for any definite
promise of an external loan, pledged upon her
assets, which were released for the purpose by
the Reparations Commission, Hungary decided,
on the advice of Sir William Goode and under
the inspiration of Count Bethlen, to proceed
immediately to the rehabilitation of her finances.
She raised an internal loan for pressing needs:
she found the capital of a bank of issue, which
was to re-establish a sound currency: she
passed all the necessary laws in a few weeks.
She signed protocols with her neighbours. She

gave every evidence that she, for her part, was determined to live in peace if her neighbours would allow her to live in peace. She is prepared to break down the custom barriers which, like the fences about English fields, render intercommunication and interchange of commodities and of ideas, so complicated in Central Europe.

One incident which illustrates the thoughtfulness of Sir William Goode and the human side of politics, may here be told. Count Bethlen and his Finance Minister were coming to Paris in connection with the preliminaries of the loan. Sir William Goode and I were to entertain them at a dinner at which a number of journalists were to be present. Now it so happened that the Finance Minister had just obtained the passage of a law prohibiting the importation into Hungary of luxuries. In his effort to prevent a further collapse of the currency, he had, for example, forbidden the introduction of fruit into Hungary. Hungary is a rich growing country but except for a small fig has little fruit of her own growing. The chief feature of our dinner, therefore, to the Prime Minister and the Finance Minister of a

country which had voluntarily decided not to
eat foreign fruit, was a huge dish containing a
compote of oranges.

The incident is not really trivial, for it serves
to point a moral and adorn a tale. That compote
of oranges was not only a little attention paid
to the Ministers but was a symbol of the little
sacrifices that Hungary was making to keep
herself from dependence upon charity. Everybody around the table appreciated the signifi-
cance of the oranges. And in what way can
a writer convey to readers the essentially human
aspect of politics than by such illustrations as
these?

Sir William Goode is still on the right side of
fifty: a handsome, clean-shaven, upright man,
with an immense store of vitality. Much as he
has done, therefore, it is more than likely that
there remain for him still bigger tasks.

When one thinks of the prominence that is
given to many politicians whose actual accom-
plishments could hardly be recalled, it will be
appreciated that Sir William Goode, who has
actually achieved this wonderful record of
having saved two countries which were otherwise fated to disappear in mere anarchy, and to

drag down a great part of the Continent with them, is a greater man than those whom we are accustomed to regard as great men. He can look back with satisfaction upon his life for he is one of those of whom it can be said that he made two blades of grass to grow where only one grew before.

He has brought hope back to millions of people. He has made peace and order possible in Central Europe.

XV

IT must be confessed that there is no figure in Germany that is thoroughly satisfactory as representing the spirit of the post-war nation. Stinnes was symbolic of much, but Stinnes is dead. Ludendorff, although acquitted triumphantly after his Bavarian escapade, is still somewhat discredited for he had been placed in a ridiculous position. Von Seeckt, though a powerful influence, does not fill the public eye. One is almost tempted to fall back upon Herr Ebert, the President of a Republic without Republicans. But the former saddler, peace-loving, happy-go-lucky, self-effacing, cannot be considered big enough. And so one could go through the whole list of Germans and not succeed in finding anybody who, interesting in himself, can be made to stand for New Germany. There are a score of names which were

known yesterday and are sadly dimmed to-day.
It would be necessary to make an effort to
recall the circumstances in which one had heard
them. Reputations come and go. Nothing is
stable in a land where everything is in flux.

Since someone must be chosen, however, let
us choose Dr. Stresemann. In spite of political
vicissitudes which carry him up or which carry
him down, Stresemann is, on the whole, the
most interesting person in the whole country.
He will disappear but he will reappear. He is
the professional politician, very able, very
cunning, very German. Doubtless he is still to
play a big part. In some respects he has disappointed expectations. When, after the occupation of the Ruhr by the French, he succeeded
to the post of Chancellor, it was thought that
he would speedily find a way out. But finding
the current against conciliation, he carefully
refrained from committing himself and thus
damaging his political future. In the end, the
man who was to have brought peace, was found
making defiant speeches, and just before the
German elections he came out plainly enough
as a Royalist. He, too, the leader of the People's
Party, would not oppose the return of the Hohen-

zollerns if that return could be accomplished without undue complications.

It may be presumed that he, too, would throw in his lot with those Germans who cry for revenge and who believe that nothing but force will solve the multiple problems which arise in Germany's relations with the neighbouring nations.

Stresemann is perhaps best described as a Lloyd George without vision. He is skilful but unscrupulous and crafty. He is an opportunist, but he cannot look far ahead. His tactlessness has been shown on many occasions. His manners are very much against him. He is rude and brusque. He will attend an appointment which he has made for midday at one-thirty and make the most perfunctory apology. Even in the Reichstag, when interrupted, he makes the most unnecessary observations, setting the Members against him. He is choleric, losing his temper over trifles. He is not what, in colloquial language, one would call a good sport. Moreover, his physical appearance is not prepossessing. It is no libel on him to say that he is ugly. Over his big lips is a small red moustache. His eyes, too, are small, and he has hardly any eyebrows. There is little hair on his head, which is square and typically Prussian.

Yet with all this he strikes one as capable of accomplishing big things, though the chances are that he would hesitate at the critical moment and play for safety. As a speaker he is fluent and persuasive. He knows English fairly well. A detail is significant. Many observers were struck with the fact that a few months ago at a dinner given by a film company which was attended by Stresemann, he wore the civilian's Iron Cross, an Imperial decoration.

It would be wrong to state that he has taken Germany further on the road to revenge, but at least he has not endeavoured to check the movement. He has followed it and he accepts most of the current German beliefs which are so dangerous for the safety of Europe. The plain truth is that the reparations problem, although it has loomed so large, is almost an incidental problem, a subsidiary problem, forming part of the much greater problem of peace and war in Europe. Germany does not accept the Treaty of Versailles which was imposed upon her against her will. Germany means sooner or later to destroy the new conditions

which obtain on the Continent. She did not
help to frame the decisions which may be held
to be unfair to her. What all men who occupy
themselves with diplomacy—and diplomacy is
not a difficult abstruse science which can only
be approached by specialists, but is the reality
of international affairs, which must touch in
some measure the lives of us all, and should be
understood by us all—what all men must be
asking themselves now is: Will there be another
war in Europe? There is much which makes for
war and it is therefore for all men to ask themselves the second question: How can war be
prevented?

It cannot any longer be denied that there are
in Germany powerful influences pushing towards
the renewal of strife. Opinions would differ
with regard to the strength of these forces, but
I suppose that in almost any company of journalists who are, after all, trained observers,
journalists who have studied the whole situation,
there would be general agreement that a war,
if not inevitable, is yet unquestionably possible
within a generation. The other day this matter
was discussed by a group of men whose business
it was to know France, and Germany, and

Poland, and other countries which will play
their part in the shaping of events. There were
in this company both Franco-philes and Franco-
phobes. There were men who believe that Germany has been badly treated and there were
men who believe, on the contrary, that Germany
has behaved both badly and stupidly. The
question was approached from many different
angles, but the unanimous verdict was that
unless a complete change for the better can be
brought about within a short time, we must
resign ourselves to the likelihood of Armageddon.

Prophecy as to dates is foolish, for they depend
upon circumstances which cannot be foreseen.
But it is noteworthy perhaps that those who
should know best gave Europe no more than
ten years' grace. Personally, I do not accept
these gloomy prognostications. It is a duty to
be cheerful, to be optimistic, to have faith in the
ultimate sanity of mankind. But one cannot
ignore the consensus of authoritative opinion,
that a situation has been created which may well
result in a more terrible upheaval than any we
have yet experienced. Realising this, it is for us
to endeavour to prevent that situation turning to
madness. Stresemann must, more than any

man, be conscious of the possibilities, and if he rises to the height of courage that is necessary, he will throw his weight on the side of peace.

It is desirable to understand the German point of view as well as the French and British points of view. If one tries to look through German eyes, one will see that treaty conditions have been made which press heavily upon Germany, not only in the material but in the moral sense. It is not only that German territory has been taken away, that a huge financial burden has been placed on the shoulders of Germany, but that Germany is smarting under a feeling of intense injustice, and, indeed, of fraud perpetrated upon her.

In the first place, it is not agreed that Germany proved herself to be militarily inferior to the Allies. Defeat came, it is contended, because President Wilson promised a peace which was afterwards denied. The majority of Germans feel that they were capable of fighting on, and if not of winning the war, at least of effecting a draw. Their good faith, they say, was deceived. The famous Fourteen Points lured them to disaster, and the famous Fourteen Points were then one by one broken.

If one would consider the mentality of Germany, it is utterly superfluous to inquire whether this propaganda is based on error or on truth. It is sufficient that it has had its effect on the German people, who are now convinced that they were improperly treated. Further, the whole case of the Allies for reparations and for measures of security, is founded upon the assumption that Germany is alone responsible for beginning the war.

It is difficult for an American or for an Englishman, and still more difficult for a Frenchman, to conceive the relative blamelessness of Germany. Has it not been proved beyond a peradventure that Germany willed the war? But we must remind ourselves that this question that has been decided in one sense in other countries, has not been so decided in Germany. The Germans, in overwhelming numbers, sincerely hold that an attempt was made to encircle them and that the war was forced upon them. If the foundations of the reconstructed Europe are thus shattered, it follows that the whole edifice falls.

To the carving up of Austria-Hungary, Germany cannot reconcile herself. But what touches her far more nearly, is the creation out of her soil of new countries, including Poland, and the occupation of German territory by the French and their Allies. A foreign army is camping in Rhineland, and shows no disposition to quit. A foreign army, illegally, even under the terms of the Treaty, say the Germans, remains in the Ruhr. To add insult to injury, it is Germany who must pay for the cost of maintenance of these foreign troops.

How is it possible for Germany to look on unmoved? She is particularly resentful of the employment of coloured troops and their alleged crimes. She has been incensed by the Separatist Movement, which she is persuaded was supported by France. She cannot but believe that France means, if not to annex the Rhine provinces, at least to cut them off from the Fatherland.

Nor can the average German be expected to admit that his government and his wealthy compatriots deliberately depreciated the mark in an attempt to escape reparation liabilities. He can only suppose that the immense sufferings through which he has passed, the incredible fluctuations of the currency, involving the greatest hardships for the ordinary German for years, are the work of those foreign forces which would reduce Germany to beggary and to subjection.

Looking around them the Germans see that France has squandered more money than is necessary for the repair of the devastated regions, and they see that France is hemming Germany in with a chain of treaties with Poland and Czecho-Slovakia and other countries. There seems no ray of hope for Germany, because even the prospect of a settlement of the reparations question would not appear to Germany to be a ray of hope, but would simply seem to be a sign of a new treaty of slavery.

Thus, owing to the oppression of the victors, Germany has been brought to a state of something like despair. There is social disorder; political passions run high; nobody has yet arisen to cope with the internal difficulties. Even Stresemann has failed; and even Stresemann feels compelled to abandon the Republic. There is a strong push towards monarchism and militarism.

But is it possible for Germany to arm against France? The folly of this method of flinging off

the French yoke is apparent to all sensible men.
It is apparent to Stresemann. In the first place,
there must be a restoration of order. There
must be economic reconstruction. There must
be better discipline. In such chaos as exists,
Germany certainly cannot fight.

With the Ruhr supervised, with the French
patrolling Rhineland, it is mere militarist madness to dream of revenge at present. But there
are Germans who pretend that, even without
the Ruhr, that great arsenal, that great work-
shop, it is possible to accumulate arms. They
have some vague thoughts of an alliance with
Russia. The diabolical ingenuity of chemists,
who direct their minds to the manufacture of
deadly gases and unknown explosives, of unthinkable potency, is not exhausted. The
inventor is pursuing a deadly work and may
transform the whole conditions of warfare in the
future.

Against the masses of Germans, who in a
comparatively few years will outnumber the
French two to one, France cannot, it is argued,
stand. There are responsible persons in Germany who do not conceal their designs. The
working-classes appear to be apathetic enough

and they may well be driven like sheep by a few active spirits. There are secret organisations everywhere under Nationalist control, and it is their business to foster the desire for revenge.

The Inter-Allied Mission for the Control of Disarmament has been flouted and nobody quite knows what preparations have been made for the fresh struggle which is beginning to be accepted as inevitable. These are grave facts, to which one cannot close one's eyes. But surely the Stresemanns of Germany will realise that nothing good can come out of the policy which is being pursued!

Nobody can estimate the consequences to civilisation if the feud between France and Germany—the only longstanding traditional quarrel left in the world—is allowed to blaze out again. Civilisation has withstood a mighty shock. Progress has been checked, if by progress one means the gradual triumph of moral ideas.

The evils which have followed in the train of the last war are apparent on every side. They are not so much the material evils. Those can be remedied very quickly. They are the spiritual evils which have overwhelmed every nation,

even the nations apparently most remote from
the battlefields. What will happen if destruction is again let loose, if the grim dogs of war
scour and ravage the earth once more? Both
materially and morally the results will be disastrous beyond dreaming. No elaboration of
this self-evident truth is needed. Everybody
with imagination must shrink appalled from the
horrors of another great conflict. But there is
no time to be lost if mankind is to be saved from
catastrophe.

Germany must be helped to choose the path
of peace and to turn from the path of war.
But it is useless to disregard the psychology of
the German nation, which is precisely as I have
endeavoured shortly to indicate it here. The
German point of view must be realised before
reconciliation can be brought about. The
tragedy is that two great European nations both
feel themselves to be in the right, both feel themselves to have been abominably treated.

The only healing organisation in the world
to-day, which is capable of bringing about a
reconciliation, is the League of Nations to which
Germany must sooner or later be admitted.
Germany, naturally, does not feel particularly

well disposed towards the League, for the League was responsible for the dubious partition of Upper Silesia. But somehow Germany must be brought in and must sit in council with France, if the age-old feud, which has scarred and devastated Europe, is to be ended.

On which side will Stresemann be found? On the side of war or on the side of peace?

Note.—The recent promise of the application of the Dawes report does not of course remove the real dangers. An economic settlement brings us up against the necessity of a political settlement. But we may now be helped over the difficult years and a new spirit be fostered in Europe.

XVI

THE POPE: AND THE REVIVAL OF THE VATICAN

RECENTLY a distinguished observer remarked to me that the most notable fact in the new Europe was not the Communist régime in Russia, was not the advent of the Labour Party in England, was not the occupation of the Ruhr by the French, but the re-emergence of the Vatican as a world power. Whether Roman Catholicism is making headway as a creed may be open to dispute, but there is no doubt that the papal influence in European chancelleries has enormously increased since the war.

For some time it was possible to ask whether Pius XI who acceded to the See of Rome in February, 1922, was to be a political Pope or an ecclesiastical Pope. The answer is now plain. Pius XI is making another bid for a great Catholic revival. He is endeavouring to extend the temporal power of the church which Cardinal

Gasparri had already, under his predecessor, striven to increase.

Personally the Pope is a particularly likable man. He is rather short in stature but his face is full of intelligence and of kindness. He is comparatively young, as Popes go. This is in itself significant, for I believe three times in succession one of the youngest Cardinals has been selected as Pope. Too often has the Pope been aged and altogether impotent. When Cardinal Ratti was chosen, there was a deliberate intention of placing in the papal chair a man who would wisely and energetically direct the church. Moreover, Cardinal Ratti knew much of European politics. He was himself a diplomatist—that is to say, he was Nuncio at Warsaw.

An Italian by birth, he is acquainted with many languages and readily talks with American or English visitors in their own tongue. He is a man who has always kept himself in good condition by his favourite sport of mountain climbing, and he still appears to be full of vigour. As he spontaneously said the other day to one of my friends in conversation, he has the highest respect for the press and has realised that it can be used even more effectively than it has yet been.

The great sign that something has changed in Vatican politics would be the deliberate exit of the Pope from the Vatican into the streets of Rome. This is I believe more than a possibility, although there are at the Vatican many "die-hards" who are horrified at the idea and are endeavouring to keep the Pope in his voluntary prison. But the Pope himself has other notions. He wishes to carry on the work of conciliation which has been begun. A little while ago it was discovered that the Pope had promised to attend a ceremony which was just outside the grounds of the Vatican. There was a tremendous uproar and at the last moment the plans were changed. It was represented that there had been some misunderstanding about the precise boundaries. The explanation was hardly convincing. It seemed as though a sort of *ballon d'essai* had been sent up, as though the Vatican was endeavouring to ascertain how the ending of the long imprisonment of the Pope would be received. There are many people who believe that next year, which is Holy Year, the Pope will, unless something intervenes, carry out his intention and cross the border line.

When the unity of the Italian Kingdom was

established fifty years ago, there were two rival
sovereigns at Rome. The Pope would not consent to the reduction of his kingdom, but it was
nevertheless forced upon him. The conditions
were never accepted by the papal authorities,
nor has the Vatican ever accepted the monetary
allowance which was made. The Italian Parliament, which in 1871 framed the law giving
independence to the spiritual power, while taking
away the temporal power of the Vatican, was
defied by the venerable Pius IX and the Pope
submitted to a kind of captivity.

Ever since that time the Vatican and the
Quirinal have existed on terms of "frozen
enmity." It appeared that the Vatican was no
longer to participate in world politics but was
to shut itself up in its own territory. Its effective power dwindled considerably. An even
worse blow than the loss of territory was the
loss of prestige in France which had been one
of the strongholds of Catholicism.

There had been unhappy incidents in the relations of France and of Rome, but on the whole
France had supported the Vatican. The power
of the priests was enormous. When the Third
Republic was formed, after the defeat of

the French by Germany, there was a strong
reaction. The priests were alleged to be anti-
Republican and the Republicans therefore became anti-Clerical. Gambetta declared open
war on the Vatican and on the priests. Jules
Simon, who became Prime Minister, brought in
anti-church legislation. Marshal MacMahon, a
Catholic President, forced Simon to quit office,
but MacMahon in his turn was quickly broken
by Parliament.

The war between clericals and anti-clericals
became exceedingly fierce in France. In 1880
Jules Ferry expelled the Jesuits. Waldeck-
Rousseau took strong disciplinary measures
against the religious orders. Emile Combes,
when he took office, became ruthless. M.
Briand disendowed the church. M. Millerand
liquidated the monasteries. It will doubtless be
remembered that the quarrel between France
and the Vatican was brought to a head by the
visit of President Loubet to the Italian King.
This was regarded as an affront to papal dignity,
for the King of Italy was a usurper, according
to ecclesiastical opinion.

If the concordat signed by Napoleon was to
be taken literally, President Loubet appears to

have been entirely in the wrong. These things are worth recalling because there is now a striking change. The Pope not only permits but encourages the visits of Catholic monarchs to Italy. In an encyclical letter which created some sensation, this point was clearly brought out, although the Pope declared that, while the antagonism between the two Italian monarchies was not to be kept alive, he surrendered nothing of papal authority; he renounced no temporal rights. He voiced once more the protests of his predecessors and demanded with even greater insistence, now that peace had been re-established between the nations, that the improper situation in which the Head of the Church was placed, should cease.

While Mussolini and Gasparri are, with the exception of occasional quarrels, on the best of terms, M. Millerand is at the Elysée in France and has been particularly prominent in affecting a reconciliation with the church. There is now at Paris a Papal Nuncio and at Rome a fully authorised French Ambassador. The "congregations" which were dispersed are returning and an agreement has recently been signed which brings peace between France and the Vatican.

The principle on which the new relations are based is the advancement of the mutual interests of the two powers. France confirms her desire to continue her traditional policy of protection of Catholics in the Orient, and claims in return the preservation of prerogatives and privileges constantly recognised by the church to official representatives of France in Palestine, in Syria, in Constantinople and all the Levant. France maintains similar rights in the Far East and in Morocco and generally wherever her interests and those of the Holy See encounter each other.

Particularly perhaps is it to be observed that in the Levant where France strives to consolidate her influence, has she need of Catholic aid, while the Vatican with its Catholic schools and other institutions, is happy to obtain French aid. A bargain has therefore been struck which has much more than local consequences. Supported by France, the Vatican is extending its power throughout Europe. Its action is of a pacifying character, and the Pope has shown a fairness towards Germany, for example, that is particularly to be commended.

It is foreshadowed that the President of the

French Republic will soon be induced to return the visit of the King of Italy that was made to the French nation and army, and it is agreed in advance that only after the President's visit to the Quirinal, proceeding from the French Embassy attached to the Holy See, will the Chief of the French State go to the Vatican; and this procedure will not be considered as constituting the least lack of courtesy towards the Holy See.

Those who are old enough to recall the intensely bitter strife of twenty or thirty years ago will realise that the wheel is turning full circle, and the Vatican after finding its political power lower than it had ever been in Europe, now finds its political power higher than it has been in modern times.

The present Pope is not alone responsible for this remarkable revival of the Vatican; but he has forwarded the movement with conspicuous skill. There is no doubt of his political bent and it is in a considerable measure owing to him that Catholicism has become a huge force that the diplomatist must reckon with everywhere. It has been helped by the upheaval in Europe, which has induced statesmen in every country to seek support wherever it can be found. They have understood that the support of the Vatican is immensely worth while, and in seeking its support they have greatly increased its power.

While governments strive, each from their own centre to control the world and become conscious that they are, in the confusion of things, almost helpless; that their writ does not run far or effectively beyond their own realm; the Vatican, which has no territorial realm, which has only a centre, has its spiritual kingdom everywhere.

Nor must it be supposed that those statesmen who desire to make use of the Vatican in world affairs are themselves members of the Roman Catholic Church. It was, I remember, Lord Balfour, who is, if he is anything, a Protestant, who asked that the moral authority of the Vatican be utilised on the League of Nations to make the League something of a reality.

So far the Vatican has taken no steps to obtain admission into the League, but, in the long run, it seems to me inevitable that a place will be found for it on the Council. It is true that the members of the League, as it was originally

conceived, are nations, and the Vatican cannot
pretend to be a nation. But the purpose of the
League is international and the Vatican claims
to be the greatest international power. It is
argued that the League is not so much an asso-
ciation of nations as an organisation placed
above the nations. Its authority is a moral
authority. Its weapons are persuasion and not
force. Surely, the Vatican, in this domain, is
a force to be reckoned with. It asserts that it is
the controlling influence in the lives of millions
of men and in the politics of many countries.
Any pronouncement made by the Pope, either
through or in alliance with the League of
Nations, might prove to be irresistible.

Pope Pius XI is perhaps, even more than his
predecessors, alive to the fact that in spite of
diplomatic blunders made during the war when
the Vatican was placed in the most unpleasant
dilemma, nothing can permanently rob the tremendous organisation of which he is the head,
of a power which, rightly directed, must be
almost invincible. There are three hundred
million adherents to the church who form a
solid block in the majority of civilised countries,
who in some cases have grouped themselves

into political parties which are **predominant.**
The church is a worldwide institution, unlike
other Christian churches, which, with the exception of the Christian Science movement,
are essentially national. The orders of Rome go
everywhere; they transcend all questions of
territory; they are transmitted from one world
centre through an endless chain of functionaries,
an unbroken hierarchy, with a traditional discipline founded upon authority.

Now, it is obvious that either for good or for
evil, in accordance with the wisdom or folly of
Vatican policy, the part it must play cannot
but be unique. In America alone there are well
over sixteen million Catholics and their numbers
have increased with extraordinary swiftness.
They are united, while the Protestant bodies
are split into scores of sects.

It may not often happen that there is a clear-
cut issue in which the church would throw the
whole weight of its influence on one side, but
if such an issue were to arise, the sixteen million
active adherents would surely turn the scales to
whichever side they pleased.

Without speaking of such essentially Catholic
countries as Spain, which hardly retain their

own power in world affairs, the Vatican's conquest of France is beyond question the most important factor in the post-war Europe. France was needed by the Vatican; and France needed the Vatican. In Middle Europe Catholicism is supreme; but there was no centralising policy until France saw her opportunity. Now French policy aims at a confederation of states along the Danube—or if federation be too big a word, let us say alliance. Rumania, Czecho-Slovakia, Jugo-Slavia, form the Little Entente. France established herself in Hungary, although Hungary was still the enemy of the Little Entente, which was, in fact, conceived and constructed in a spirit of fear of Hungary. Somehow France manages to reconcile this contradiction.

With Austria France is friendly. There was a moment when France even endeavoured to enter into special relations with Catholic Bavaria. Probably the Middle Europe policy of France can never be accomplished as it was conceived by M. Paléologue, but if it is now not so diagrammatic as it was originally, the idea nevertheless persists of using Catholicism for the consolidation of the jig-saw Middle Europe.

Poland, too, is Catholic, and Poland is one of

the "friends in the East" which Marshal Pétain
has declared to be necessary. The return of
Alsace-Lorraine to France helps in this new
orientation towards Rome, for Alsace-Lorraine
are faithful Catholic provinces. But in Germany proper an attempt is being made to work
on the Catholic sentiments of the South as
against Protestant Prussia.

Everything, indeed, makes for a revival of
Catholicism and of the Vatican as one of the
greatest influences in European diplomacy. It
would be strange if the Pope and his advisers
did not make some use of this situation, if the
Curia did not embark on an ambitious international policy. Mr. Sefton Delmer has shown
how the dream of Pope Leo XIII of restoring
the moral hegemony of the Papacy by means
of speculative encyclicals remained unrealised,
and how Pope Pius X in his honest but naïve
battle against science and the "corrosive modern
spirit" still further weakened the bastions of the
Vatican. But Pope Benedict XV, with Cardinal
Gasparri, a new Rampolla, at his side, strove to
reach the goal of Leo XIII, not by an appeal to
the philosophic and learned, but by an appeal
to the same audience as that addressed by the

politicians. He endeavoured to capture the Labour movement for the church.

The present Pope Pius XI, has taken another course. He sees the advantage of employing diplomacy to achieve his purpose. The ramifications of this policy could be discovered everywhere.

I have endeavoured to be neither the critic nor the propagandist, but to set down impartially the truth about the revival of the Vatican under Pius XI. Whether it is good or bad for the world that this immense organisation should have temporal power, should be immixed in diplomacy, is an intensely controversial subject, on which I refrain from pronouncing in one way or the other. But that the Roman Catholic Church is more conscious than ever of its might, moral and political, is certain, and no survey of the personalities that matter in Europe would be complete without this reference to the man who has brought into the world in a more vivid way a new, or rather, a new-old force, which is perhaps more noteworthy, more important, than any other phenomenon in the Europe of to-day.

Note.—The triumph of the Radicals in France may totally destroy many of the diplomatic calculations of the Vatican. The French Radicals are essentially anti-clerical.

XVII

GENERAL SIKORSKI: POLAND'S ARMY CHIEF

POLAND has an army of three hundred thousand men. She professes that she cannot reduce the number. It is such facts as these that help to make America suspicious of Europe and cause her to hold aloof. What can these large armies, maintained by comparatively small States, and, above all, by States which have in the past been oppressed and which now show a tendency themselves to oppress, signify, if they do not signify the militarist mentality? If all through Central Europe one finds a number of countries each with troops which exceed the strength of the American or the British armies, what can one conclude but that the materials of war are being piled up and must some day be used again? Nevertheless, an injustice would be done to Poland if this conclusion were accepted too lightly and without explanation.

Probably the most important person in Poland is General Sikorski, who is the Minister of War. He is a fine handsome fellow, tall, upstanding, with an air of determination, with undoubted intelligence, and with a real appreciation of the position in which Poland finds herself after her resurrection. The history of Poland has been the history of the repeated partition of Poland. Will the country again be sliced up between Russia and Germany? She has two of the most powerful nations, one on either side, both of them believing that Poland has grown at the expense of her neighbours, both of them awaiting the propitious moment to recover territory which they profess is not Polish but is either German or Russian.

To avoid being crushed between these two forces, Poland, to whom her friends have been perhaps too kind, since they have made her bigger than is good for her, will have to exercise a most cautious diplomacy. She must frankly go out to make peace with one or the other of her neighbours and, if possible, with both. But in the meantime, according to the conception of General Sikorski, she must keep her army in a high state of efficiency.

The Polish army, far from being efficient in the early stages, was a menace to Poland herself. When the Bolsheviks fought it in 1920 they drove it back to the very gates of Warsaw and would undoubtedly have entered Warsaw had not the French gone to the assistance of Poland and enabled the army to rally and force back the Bolsheviks. Since then the French officers have helped to place the Polish army on a better footing and, indeed, there is a military alliance, which is perhaps open to criticism, between Poland and France.

Poland has apparently placed her hopes on France, and France in turn has founded her foreign policy on Poland as the key-State of the Continent. Possibly it will in the long run not be a good thing for Poland to be regarded by Germany and by Russia as the watch-dog of France. In any case, General Sikorski defends his country from the charge of militarism. It is not because Poland is aggressive but because she is conscious of the necessity of defending herself that she holds herself in readiness for any emergency.

When all is said and done, there has been some improvement. Under General Pilsudski, the

Polish army was twice as large. Poland has now thirty infantry divisions, each of three regiments, and ten cavalry brigades. All Poles are pledged to serve for two years, but recently Sikorski has, in consequence of the unsettled economic conditions, granted what is called the "agricultural leave of absence." It is not perhaps sufficiently realised what a tremendous drain on a country's resources is a large conscript army. There is not only the direct cost of the soldiers' keep but there must be reckoned their withdrawal from useful work. Now, if Poland is to consolidate herself, all her citizens should be profitably employed. Sikorski has at least this merit, that he has, in spite of his conviction that a large army is needed, also considered the necessity of cultivating the soil and has released as many men as possible for this purpose.

When the war against Russia was being prosecuted, there were actually under arms nearly one million men. It might be supposed that the volunteers of that time would be released from compulsory service. This is not the case. Sikorski has improved the standard of training and he desires that even those who have fought shall pass through the reorganised army, in order that the military man-power of Poland shall be brought up to a uniform level. Moreover, a complete register of members of the reserve forces is required. It is argued that Poland will thus be able at almost any moment to mobilise on a war strength. Her citizens of military age will all have passed through the course of training and will all be available whenever they are wanted. Thus it may be said that the peace army is only a nucleus. As Sikorski puts it, the sole duty of an army in peace time is to train.

Whatever may be the numerical strength of the active army, the War Minister is endeavouring to teach the largest possible number of Poles the trade of soldiering. At least Sikorski is carrying out his conceptions with skill. The new Polish army is certainly well trained and is fairly well equipped. It lacks some of the more modern weapons, such as tanks and aeroplanes. Poland is poor: Poland cannot afford these technical means. Therefore, in spite of the good opinion of such men as Marshal Foch, who recently inspected the Polish army, and in spite of the soldierly qualities of the men, it may be doubted whether Poland could resist a strong attack directed by a State which is armed with the newer kinds of weapons. In spite of the intensive training of the whole nation, General Sikorski is still anxious. Naturally, the Polish army is largely modelled on that of the French, but the training in tactics is somewhat different. Chiefly the Polish experience has been on the Eastern fronts where fighting has hitherto been of a somewhat different character from that of the Western fronts.

Sikorski holds that the disarmament idea of the League of Nations is fallacious, in that although it would reduce military forces under arms in peace time, it would not reduce the potential number of men who in time of war could be put into the field. Now, in Germany, whose army has been restricted, nominally at least, by the Treaty of Versailles, neither the Allies acting under the Treaty nor the League acting under any scheme which may hereafter be adopted, can change the hard fact that a large proportion of the men who fought during the Great War will for a considerable time to come be able to fight again if the occasion arises. Peace time strength is misleading.

But there is this to be said, on the other hand,
that Germany is not allowed to pass new classes
through a military training school. She cannot
conscript. She must recruit her army on a long
service basis. Even this law is, however, made
to be broken, and there is reason to believe that
unauthorised drilling in one form or another is
being practised.

As for the Russians, they come under no
international law of any kind. They are at
present untouched by the League. Disarmament must be general or it is useless and worse
than useless. But at the same time is armament, for a country placed as Poland is placed,
really useful? Would not Poland be swamped
whatever Sikorski did or left undone, were there
to be once more a general upheaval in Europe?
If peace is not assured to Poland, she will never
right herself economically. Thus, she is living
a precarious life, economically unsound, in-
adequately protected in the military sense. It
is only by a general arrangement, only by common goodwill, that Poland will become viable.

It is as well, however, to endeavour to understand the painful dilemma which faces Sikorski.
Knowing as he knows that if the moment were

favourable Germany could call up an army of several million men, that Russia could throw more millions into the field against Poland, he has reason to fear for Polish independence, and he cannot, as a soldier and as the War Minister, consent to further reduction of the Polish forces.

It is not easy for America, which cannot be attacked by another country, to realise the problem which confronts Sikorski. It is not easy for England, surrounded by the sea, to appreciate his state of mind. Even a country like Spain is separated from France by the Pyrenees, a natural frontier which can hardly be crossed. Poland has a long frontier which is ill-defined, which is without natural protection. Poland has straggled out into Russian territory. She has, to use a colloquialism, bitten off more than she can chew.

No wonder that all the new nations in Europe are obsessed by the fear of attack. They are built upon no solid foundations. They clamour for the general recognition of the existing frontiers, but that general recognition is not likely to be given. Take the opinion in Germany. German opinion, according to the best observers, demands rectifications of the Polish frontiers, which were summed up by a writer in the London "Nation" as follows:

1. The complete abolition of the Polish corridor to Dantzig which now divides Germany in two.

This point was illustrated by a German as follows: "It is as if a strip of Irish Free State territory were placed between England and Scotland to give Ireland access to the German Ocean." East Prussia is now detached from the rest of Germany, and East Prussia chafes, while the rest of Germany is resentful.

2. The readjustment of the Upper Silesian frontiers and the return to Germany of Marienburg and other Polish districts.

The League of Nations is not forgiven for the division of Upper Silesia, which favoured Poland unduly.

Germany would, of course, require readjustments which do not, however, particularly concern Poland. There is, for example, the problem of the Sarre. There is the demand for the evacuation of the territories occupied by the French and their Allies. Into these matters it is unnecessary to go again, as it is unnecessary to go into the possibility of a return of Colonial territory in East Africa and elsewhere if the danger of war is to be averted.

But if these questions do not directly touch Poland, indirectly they affect her position very seriously. For a war between France and Germany probably involves a war between Germany and Poland. It does not much matter in the practical sense whether a war begins over Germano-Polish frontiers or as the result of a Franco-German quarrel. The result will be precisely the same for Poland.

It may be recalled, too, that when the Conference of Ambassadors recognised Poland's Eastern frontier as defined in the Treaty of Riga, it referred to the line as "the frontier established by Poland and Soviet Russia on their own responsibility." The Allies would seem, therefore, to disclaim any contractual or moral obligation to defend this frontier. It was not Sikorski who created this unfortunate situation, nor can he alter it. He has to deal with the existing facts and he cannot be blamed for dealing with them as a military man, even though he is aware of the insufficiency of any preparations that he is able to make. One may

doubt the wisdom of establishing Poland on
Polish and French military strength, but what
other course, asks Sikorski, could be taken?

Rightly directed, Poland is destined to play
a great part in the New Europe. The country,
by numbers, history and extent, is unquestionably at the head of the hierarchy of peoples
which have been created or modified from the
Baltic to the Adriatic. It cannot help coming
under French influence. The French cannot
help regarding it as a rampart—as a boulevard
between Germany and Russia. It is really the
key-State of Europe. If true peace can be made
at Warsaw, Europe is safe. But if not, Europe
will flounder uneasily on for a few years, only to
be plunged at the end into a perilous morass.

There have been some remarkable persons
engaged in the remaking of this State. There
was Paderewski who left the piano to become
the representative of Poland at the Paris Peace
Conference. There was General Pilsudski, who
was the President of the Republic, and who may
perhaps be regarded as the real creator of Poland. His name may be written in history side
by side with the name of Kosciusko. He came
out of the German gaol of Magdeburg, having

repulsed with scorn the German offer of autonomy.   He raised legions which constituted the
new national army, now directed by Sikorski.
With ill-shod, ill-clad, ill-nourished troops, in
whom he had inspired his own heroic faith, he
fought on all the borders of Poland, against
the Bolsheviks, against the Germans, against
the Ukranians, against invaders on every side.
His military performance was prodigious.

The sympathy of America and of the Allied
peoples could not but go out to the Poles, who, in
their bondage had clung tenaciously to the hope
of restoration, feeding their faith on historical
memories, fostering in adverse circumstances
their love of liberty.   Their legitimate aspirations could not be denied.   But the danger of
the sentimental feelings which possessed the
peacemakers, as was natural, was that they led
us away from realities, that they caused the
most inflated claims to be recognised, even
though those claims may eventually lead to
Poland's undoing.

Poland even made demands in Lithuania
instead of trying to live on peaceful terms with
the Lithuanians and of constructing a confederation of the smaller Baltic States.   She asked for

great tracts of land, which beyond question are Russian, and she encroached on Germany, heedless of the consequences.

It would be an exceedingly bad thing for Europe if little State after little State were to die out like the morning street lamps at the passing of the lamplighter. The conception of a *Pologne Forte* was encouraged by the Quai d'Orsay. In the end there was a huge patched-up Poland which cannot but induce doubts. Strength is a word which has been much misunderstood; for strength does not come from extent but from justice and homogeneity.

Poland, at present, has about twenty-seven million inhabitants. Several millions are of German origin and several millions are of Russian origin. There are also several million Jews. The country is formed of the three parts of Poland which belonged before the war to Russia, to Austria, and to Prussia.

It is a country which, if it is given a fair chance, must become prosperous. Its natural riches are considerable. Its agricultural produce is not only sufficient to nourish its entire population, but there is a surplus which might be exported. The latest figures show that Poland ought to be able to export each year twelve million quintals of wheat, and the same quantity of potatoes, besides six thousand waggons of eggs. Large quantities of sugar could also be exported. Poultry, cattle, horses and so forth, can also be sent out of the country.

There is, however, an agrarian movement which is somewhat alarming. The peasants are demanding the possession of the soil. Industrially also Poland is wealthy. She has great quantities of coal. There is iron, salt, potash in profusion. In Galacia there is petroleum. An important textile industry should be developed. Unhappily, there is at present much mismanagement and, further, many of the external markets are closed to Poland. This is notably the case of the Russian market. The problem of competent administration is difficult. The Prussian officials did not understand the Polish language. The Russian functionaries returned to Russia. The Austrian administrators remained but in insufficient numbers. Protégés of Polish politicians were employed but many of them were incapable. Traffic on the railways is not half that of the pre-war days, and the railways are worked at a loss by the State. The State is a large owner in Poland. It possesses vast forests and hundreds of mills. It owns mines, controls the telephones, has a tobacco monopoly, and so forth. And whether this is to be used as an argument against State control or not, one is bound to remark that the State industries and exploitations have so far resulted disastrously.

The Polish finances are extremely bad. There is no proper budget; that is to say, the budget is left unbalanced and Polish marks are emitted to make up the deficit. This deficit last year amounted to 600 milliard marks. In order to compare the Polish taxes with those of France, one should translate the payments into gold francs. On this basis, the Polish taxpayer pays 18 gold francs a year as compared with 250 francs paid by the French. It will be seen that there must be a complete reorganisation of Poland and that foreign aid is necessary if the country is to convert its potential prosperity into realities. The Poles are a proud people. They have lost their independence for so long that they are afraid of foreign aid, which nevertheless is indispensable. But if foreign capital is undoubtedly needed, foreign capital is shy.

The Prime Minister, M. Granski, is struggling gallantly with the fiscal problems which beset the new State. Still, to me the central figure in Poland is that of General Sikorski, for before there can be prosperity in Poland there must be security.

Is Sikorski taking the right path?

XVIII

MUSTAPHA KEMAL: THE NAPOLEON OF THE NEW TURKEY

CAN Mustapha Kemal Pasha be counted among the Europeans? Strictly speaking, he has made himself a non-European and has passed over into Asia. The New Turkey, with a mere foothold at Constantinople in Europe, has gone out into Anatolia, and in its pride takes up a hostile attitude towards Europe and things European. Constantinople, the old capital of Turkey, is regarded by Angora, the new capital of Turkey, as a mere nest of traitors. Constantinople has become, for the Nationalist Turks, contaminated by contact with the Western peoples. Its population is Greek, Jewish, Rumanian, with a mixture of the Western races—it is not a truly Turkish city as is Angora.

The Powers talked for a long time of ejecting Turkey from Europe—"bag and baggage" was the Gladstonian phrase—but although they allowed Turkey to remain in Europe, Turkey herself has gone over into Asia by the ferry steamer starting from the Galata pier—and the Bosphorus divides the European and the Asiatic shores.

But somehow the picture of Europe would not be complete if one did not squeeze into one corner a bit of Anatolia. Without discussing therefore whether Turkey in Asia is a piece of Europe in Asia, or whether Turkey in Europe is a piece of Asia in Europe, we will include in our gallery the figure of Mustapha Kemal.

Mustapha Kemal is generally represented as a particularly fine handsome man, soldierly in appearance, with a commanding presence, ruling the Turks with a rod of iron. But this description is scarcely accurate. Mustapha Kemal with his asymmetrical face, with his nervous movements, is not at all impressive. There is among the men of Angora a real reaction against the Byzantine splendours of Constantinople. They are simple folk, the men of Angora, and their residences and meeting-places are not at all sumptuous. They gather round their stoves, muttering parrot phrases against the foreigner.

A dingy, muddy, uncouth town is Angora, and throughout Anatolia primitive conditions prevail.

Mustapha Kemal may stand out against this background of fanatics as a comparatively wise, sober and moderate man. His influence is certainly a restraining influence, but it would be inadvisable for him to press his authority too far. He gave his name to the Nationalist Movement. His followers, who revolted against the Treaty of Sèvres, were known as Kemalists. It was the Kemalists who began, continued, and ended the war for independence. It was the Kemalists who stampeded the Greeks. It was the Kemalists who frightened the great Western Powers. It was the Kemalists who, when invited by the great Western Powers to tear up the Treaty of Sèvres which had been accepted by the Sultan with his seat at Constantinople, and was regarded by Angora as the craven symbol of Turkish defeat—it was the Kemalists who at Lausanne stated their terms to the great Western Powers and imposed upon the great Western Powers another Treaty which registered the defeat of the Allies.

There has rarely been such a reversal of fortunes in so short a space of time. If Germany had endeavoured to scrap the Treaty of Versailles and had tried to frame in its own way another Treaty with the Allies, one knows that Germany would have absurdly failed. But what was not possible for Germany was possible for an apparently insignificant group of men who in Angora raised the banner of defiance, even though the Allied soldiers were camping in Constantinople and the Chief of the Turkish State was virtually the prisoner of the Allies. It seemed grotesque to pit this dwarf against the giants. But the Kemalists knew that they could not be seriously hurt by the Allies, who were quarrelling among themselves, and who could not in face of public opinion in their countries, raise troops to fight another fight. Mustapha Kemal and his followers knew that they could harass the Allies. This was their plan and it is not surprising that with its success Mustapha Kemal has a certain ascendancy over the Turks. But this ascendancy is purely relative and he must now, sometimes against his better judgment, follow his followers rather than insist upon his followers following him.

Eventually the Allies (or rather the British,

for the French, preoccupied with other problems, quickly gave their sympathies to the Turks) launched the Greek armies against the Kemalists. It was a fatal mistake. The Greeks made some progress but the Turks merely fell back and bided their time. At last they broke the Greek armies completely. The Greek armies were driven to the coast. There was rejoicing in France, where the anti-Greek sentiment which had persisted throughout the war after the treacherous conduct of King Constantine, now expressed itself openly.

The British might have hung on had they not been deserted at Chanak, but they could have accomplished very little. Sooner or later the growing resistance of the Turks of Angora must have resulted in victory. It could not be overcome unless an expedition on a large scale were possible.

But even in England, where anti-Turkish feeling had in some circles, ever since the days of Gladstone, reached almost a religious fervour, there was a serious division of opinion. The idea of a new war in far-off parts for a cause which did not appeal to the average Englishman, was fiercely rejected. The downfall of

Lloyd George was determined by many considerations, but by nothing more than the reluctance of the British people to be led into strife.

Thus the cards were all in the hands of Mustapha Kemal, and it must be confessed that he played them with real skill. When a new peace was offered, however, he (or rather the Grand Assembly at Angora) was inclined to push his advantage, which was an advantage of circumstances, somewhat too far. The Turkish demands grew greater and greater. They were supported by the French and in the end the Turks obtained their own way on almost every point.

Lord Curzon tried to put the best face on it all, but the diplomatic defeat which he suffered must have been particularly galling to the ex-Viceroy of India. One cannot refrain from expressing some regret at the attitude of the French who helped to place the Allies in the most humiliating position. What has been their reward? Although the Kemalists can cherish no affection for the British, they have for them some respect. But for the French, who have been their friends, they have none. The French have been worse treated, both at Constantinople and in Anatolia, since the completion of the victory of Mustapha Kemal, than have the British. M. Franklin Bouillon, whose pro-Turkish policy it was which led the French into these errors, had his moment of triumph but he is now discredited as a statesman.

Is it not amazing that Mustapha Kemal, apparently without means of action, should thus have won against the great Powers the independence of Turkey? There has rarely been such a turning of the tables. What is now curious is that the Turks should continue to prefer such a ramshackle little capital as Angora, which has served its purpose, to the beautiful and ancient city of Constantinople. But Constantinople will never be in the eyes of the Kemalists the city that it was. It has been soiled and ruined morally by the part it played in the Turkish fight for freedom.

The Kemalists, nearly two years ago, abolished the Sultanate but they preserved the Caliphate. Now they have deposed the Caliph. They will not recognise even a spiritual chief who shall sit in state in Constantinople.

Angora has grown arrogant. The New Turkey

believes that it can stand alone and repudiates
not only all international solidarity with the
Christians, but even with the Mussulman
peoples. A wave of xenophobia has swept from
Angora to the shores of the Bosphorus. There
is a wild national enthusiasm, an almost childish
vanity. The Turkish newspapers are unanimous
in their opposition to other nations. They may
be compelled to receive the assistance of foreign
capital, but for the present they feel they can
suffice unto themselves. Particularly do they
show their animosity towards the French Catholic schools. They appear to ascribe all their
misfortunes of the past twenty years to these
schools. It is the foreigner who is responsible
for the financial difficulties and for the disorganisation of the Ottoman administration.

would be a mistake to suppose that the
New Turkey is merely the prey of religious
fanaticism. It is a nationalist sentiment and
not religious sentiment that is uppermost.
Islam itself means less than ever to the Turks.
Secularism has made immense strides. Religion may not have been altogether deposed
with the Caliphate, but it has much less sway
than ever before. Turkey, which may be said

to be passing through another period of youth is beginning to mock even those things which have been traditionally held to be sacred.

It must be noted, too, that reforms, real reforms, are being effected. The Turkish woman is rejecting the veil and has received the vote. The Turkish woman, regarded in the West as the mere slave of the man, is becoming free. It is already astonishing to think of Turkey as a Republic; but it is still more astonishing to think of the Turkish woman as enjoying a liberty as great as that enjoyed in America or in England.

In all these later developments the part that Mustapha Kemal has played is somewhat doubtful. There was a time when he might have himself aspired to the Caliphate and have become a new Mohammed. He has shown a good deal of hesitation and is hardly the leader of supreme power that he might have become. On the whole, he has tried to be a moderating influence and has been outpassed. When once people like the Turks begin to break with tradition, they are bound to go much further than could ever have been expected of them, and Mustapha Kemal seems to have lagged in the rear. It is quite possible that within a few years he will be displaced.

The Allied Powers are now preparing to set up their Embassies, not at Constantinople that great and glorious city which has one of the best sites in the world, but in the remote, inconvenient, tumbledown little place known as Angora. Surely it would have been better to have forgotten after Lausanne the foolish rivalry between Constantinople and Angora, which although perhaps justified during the storm and stress of the struggle, is ridiculous in present circumstances.

One wonders what would have happened had the Sultan stood up against the hostility of the Kemalists and have refused to quit Constantinople. Instead of flying in a British ship, he might have asserted his authority. The course of events would have been undoubtedly different, for at that moment the revolution against the palace had not become so strong as it was bound to become when the Sultan practically deposed himself. But we must take things as they are. The most advanced revolutionaries have won.

What will now follow? The tide will go back.

For materially Turkey is not in good condition. She needs many good harvests to return to even relative prosperity. Although she has successfully overcome the Allies, although she has effected startling reforms, she cannot seriously pretend to be treated permanently as a great modern Power. She has a long way to go beofre she reaches the intellectual standards of the West. There are elaborate programmes of reconstruction, but they are not being realised. The great want is money and it is difficult to see how Mustapha Kemal, with all his qualities of leadership, can consolidate the Republic which he has set up with himself as President.

One excellent observer, Mr. Maxwell Macartney, rightly doubts whether Turkey is ripe for a prosperous Republic. The proclamation, he says, was staged without any open and adequate discussion in the Assembly. With all the mouthing of fine phrases by the mumbling men around their stoves, Turkey cannot be regarded as a European Democracy. Kemal Pasha, for example, combined with the Presidency of the State, the Presidency of the Assembly, of the Cabinet, and of the Popular Party. This was an extraordinary accumulation of power; but in reality, his power was nothing like so effective as might be judged by his multiple offices.

In short, it is as yet far too early to predict what will be the ultimate outcome of the chances and changes of the past few years. It is a strange paradox that those who wish to return to a more orthodox state of affairs should be clustered in Constantinople, while the reformers should be found in the little towns and in the countryside of Anatolia. Generally, the radical elements are to be found in the big towns and the conservative elements in the country. It is just because of this paradox that one wonders whether the present régime can last. The situation is abnormal. It is the result of ten years of practically continuous warfare. From whatever angle one approaches the problem of Turkey, one comes back to the antagonism of Constantinople and of Angora. Nothing that has yet happened has really altered that fundamental division of Turkey.

While men like Mustapha Kemal seem to believe that the future of Turkey lies outside Europe, there are others who still believe that the future of Turkey must be based upon a power which has elected its home in the one adequate city which is on the European side. As an Asiatic nation Turkey will be handicapped. Turkey will remain a backward power. The present conceptions are surely ephemeral. In the modern world xenophobia is a disease. It is a disease which may prove to be fatal. At the best it will prevent progress. It is against the whole notion of civilisation.

Nobody nowadays wants to drive the Turks out of Europe. On the contrary, it might be better for the world if the barriers which have separated East and West were broken down and Turkey were to come into greater contact with the European nations. Certainly the old conditions can never be restored. That is in itself a good thing; for they, too, made for insularity and mutual incomprehension. But in some modified form there seems to be no reason why a compromise should not be made between the insularity of Angora and the insularity of Constantinople — for although Constantinople was superficially the most cosmopolitan city in the world, it yet remained with its institutions a truly narrow and nationalist centre.

Strangely enough, the Turks have never, in spite of the international mingling of Constanti-

nople, ever lived on intimate terms with real
Europeans.   There is no reason why they
should not.   They are able and courteous, and
are perhaps properly regarded by those who
have lived among them as the gentlemen of the
Balkans.   They have, of course, committed
the most terrible atrocities, largely because of
their religious fanaticism.   Now that this fanaticism is disappearing, it will surely not be permanently replaced by a nationalist fanaticism.

The future of Turkey therefore depends very
largely on whether the present Nationalism is a
passing phase: whether Turkey is prepared to
take its rightful place among civilised peoples.
Now Mustapha Kemal has done well in bringing the Turks out of bondage; but has he led
them into a bondage which in the end will be
even worse?

There is reason to believe that Mustapha
Kemal is himself disposed to check the terrible
tendency towards xenophobia which may ruin
the New Turkey.   There is reason to believe
that he will endeavour, for his part, when things
have settled down again, to make fresh contacts
and to make of the Turkish nation, not a mere
Ishmael, but a modern civilisation.

XIX

DR. DORTEN: THE RHINELANDER AT HOME

DR. DORTEN, perhaps more than any man in Europe, stands for an idea. He represents the idea of the independence of Rhineland. It may prove to be that there is no more important idea, whether disruptive or constructive, working in Europe to-day.

It was in Paris that I first met Dr. Dorten. This German had come to the French capital to interest Monsieur Poincaré, if possible, in the Rhineland movement. But M. Poincaré was extremely cautious. He declined to see Dorten and one of the bitterest complaints that Dorten made to me as he adjusted his eyeglass was that while he was, in spite of German obloquy, striving for the virtual separation of the Rhineland provinces from the rest of the Reich, he could obtain comparatively little support in France. He felt this as a grievance.

The hand of the Germans is turned against him and if ever the French evacuate the territories along the Rhine, which they occupied in virtue of the provisions of the Treaty, Dorten will doubtless be treated as a traitor by the German authorities.

Why, then, were the French authorities not more sympathetic? The position of Dorten seemed to me to be pitiful. Nobody wanted him and the attempt to shake off the Prussian yoke did not appear to have much immediate prospect of success. Nevertheless, there do exist in Rhineland forces which make for separation, and even though the cause has a temporary setback it may yet triumph. No idea which is rooted in necessity ever really dies.

Dr. Dorten himself is a man who strikes one as being perfectly sincere and by no means the adventurer who is working for money or even for personal prestige. He talks with great volubility and repeats his arguments with countless variations as one who is completely master of his subject. He is rather short in stature, is clean shaven, and wears an enormous eye-glass which gives him a somewhat foppish air.

One cannot quite picture him leading an
attack on a town hall. It is hardly by violence
that the Rhinelanders will ever effect their
independence. It will be by political combina-
tions and by diplomatic intrigues. Although
Dr. Dorten has not hesitated to face danger
and is perpetually in a perilous position, it is
on the protection of the French that he chiefly
relies for the accomplishment of the task he has
set himself. It must not be imagined that this
task is hopeless. There are powerful arguments
which Dr. Dorten used which appeal to certain
sections of the Rhineland peoples and he is not
without special means of ultimately achieving
his purpose.

When the French local authorities in Rhineland appeared to favour the Rhineland movement, there was a great outcry in England,
and indeed in America. The unity of the Reich
is regarded by the majority of people in almost
every country as sacred. The break-up of
Germany would be considered a disastrous
thing or, at any rate, an immoral thing.

The external forces against Dorten and the
idea he represents are extremely strong. Even
in France, there is no enthusiasm for him or for

his idea. The risks of failure are too great for
any ordinary diplomatist to commit himself.
A few men like General Mangin, who is possessed
of extraordinary political courage as well as of
military courage, unreservedly declare that they
want to detach the Rhineland from the Reich.
Marshal Foch, too, is known to be in favour of
making the Rhine the frontier of Germany, and
the Rhinelands on the left bank of the river a
sort of a buffer state between France and Germany.

The military men, indeed, are much bolder
than the politicians in France. The politicians
want security but they are not prepared to
come out openly for this particular method of
obtaining security. M. Poincaré, when he was
President of the Republic, is known to have
written a letter—it was, in fact, published in a
recent Yellow Book—urging the continuous
occupation of Rhineland until absolute guarantees of the safety of France could be obtained.
There is only one kind of absolute guarantee
which is believed to be effective, and that is, the
recognition of the Rhine as the frontier of Germany. This does not mean that the Rhine is
also the frontier of France. It does not mean

that the French should annex the Rhineland
provinces; it means simply that the Rhineland
provinces should have an autonomous existence.
At the back of all French minds is the desire,
more or less vague, rarely expressed with clear-
ness, for the separation of Rhineland. The
desire is an old one. One could trace it back
for many generations. It seems to have haunted
Napoleon. Chateaubriand certainly advocated
it. Rhineland is, as it were, a jumping-off
ground for a German invasion of France, and
the French live in constant fear of a new German
invasion, as they have lived for at least a century.

The idea is to be found in an attenuated form
in the actual arrangements, which were made
during the Peace Conference in Paris in 1919,
for the Allied occupation of the left bank of the
Rhine. Although this occupation is often put
forward as constituting a means of pressure on
Germany to ensure the payment of reparations,
its real *raison d'être* is the instinct of security.
While the French are in Rhineland they feel
that Germany cannot attack them.

But the Treaty provides for their evacuation
of this territory fifteen years after the application

of Versailles. Indeed, this evacuation is to be effected in stages every five years. Five years after the application of the Treaty, a section of Rhineland should be left by the French— or Allied—troops. In the tenth year another section must be left. In the fifteenth year Rhineland must be entirely freed from French troops.

But there is a provision in the Treaty by which the French may ignore this arrangement. It is clearly stated that if Germany does not fulfil her obligations or if the Allies are not satisfied with the guarantees which are given at the end of this period of occupation they may continue to keep their armies in Rhineland. This is tantamount, according to the French inter-pretation; to a right to remain in perpetuity. Moreover, the French seem inclined to avail themselves of this proviso. Next year the whole question may arise in an acute form, for the first five years will have run their course in January, 1925. Germany will ask for the partial evacuation of her territories. The French will doubtless refuse to comply with this request. Unless there is some settlement of a permanent character this year, there cannot fail to be further international debates of a somewhat grave kind.

Now the Rhinelanders appreciate their uncomfortable situation between the Berlin Government and the Paris Government. They realise that they are between the hammer and the anvil. It is about them that the dispute will rage. They are naturally anxious to get rid of the French occupation, but they are not anxious to come under Prussian rule. Hence their wish for a separate life of their own. They are—so runs the argument—neither French nor German—or, at least, they are a very special kind of German: they are Rhinelanders.

Those who have the merest smattering of history know that the Franks made France. It is the Franks who gave their very name to France. After the break-up of Rome, after the Gallo-Roman régime in France, the Gauls, practically deserted by their protectors, were in danger of being overrun by various barbaric peoples. It was to the Franks that they looked and the Franks, seizing their opportunity, helped to create the modern France.

Now the Franks came from the Rhineland

territories. There can be little doubt that there are certain affinities between the Rhinelanders and the French. But, on the other hand, the Franks were of Germanic stock and they have been incorporated in the greater Germany which has arisen and which was consolidated into the German Empire by Bismarck.

Far be it from me to suggest that the Rhinelanders are not in a certain sense good Germans. But they are not quite the same kind of Germans as the Germans from beyond the Rhine. How far they are conscious of their difference is probably a matter of opinion. How deep is the desire for separation is a subject of endless controversy. Whether Dr. Dorten would have made the smallest progress without the presence of the French in Rhineland is open to dispute. The best evidence which I can gather would seem to show that Dr. Dorten is in a minority. But that there exists a genuine movement which has not been unduly stimulated by the political activities of the French, appears to me to be beyond doubt.

Dr. Dorten, as he has explained the case of the Rhinelanders, who think with him, in conversations with me, believes that it will be partic-

ularly unfortunate for Rhineland if there should
be another war between Germany and France.
And this war in present circumstances appears
to many observers to be almost inevitable. That
is why the French will certainly not relinquish
their grip on Rhineland until they are entirely
reassured. Therefore the battleground of the
next war will not be France, will not be Germany proper, but will be the Rhineland. The
Rhineland will be devastated. Whichever side
wins, Rhineland will lose. It is not difficult to
understand the anxiety of the inhabitants of
this region. Why should their land be the cock-
pit of the two contending forces which perpetuate
the only traditional feud in Europe? The Rhinelanders do not want another war for they will
be the unhappy victims. They are, therefore,
out of sympathy with Prussia. But it does
not necessarily follow that they are in full
sympathy with France. Men like Dr. Dorten
are disposed to cry, "A plague on both your
houses."

Would not the possibilities of war be gradually
lessened, they ask, if Rhineland were free, if
Rhineland were neutralised in a real sense? On
the whole, the Rhinelanders are a peaceful

people. They are not aggressive like the Prussians, but they do not relish the prospect of a French occupation of which the end cannot be foreseen.

Men like Maurice Barrès advocated a Rhineland policy which consisted in the extension of French influence in the territories on the left bank of the river, for it is undoubtedly true, as I have indicated, that the Frenchmen of the East and the Germans of the West are not altogether dissimilar. Unfortunately, the French occupying authorities, instead of cultivating friendships in Rhineland, have behaved tactlessly. Barrès would have employed intellectual methods: the occupying authorities have employed military methods.

When in the stress of war the constituent elements of the ramshackle Austro-Hungarian Empire broke apart, the Allies did not hesitate to espouse the cause of Czecho-Slovakia and of the Southern Slavs. Czecho-Slovakia is today an ally of France. Yugo-Slavia belongs to the Little Entente, which has thrown in its lot with France. The example has appealed to Dr. Dorten. He does not see why the Rhineland provinces should not become, as it were, a second Czecho-Slovakia. But the analogy cannot be pushed very far. The Czechs and the Slovaks had striven for their liberty long before the war. During the war they fought on the side of the Allies. Their propaganda was one of the factors which contributed to the winning of the war by the Allies. They were oppressed peoples who were always in a state of incipient revolt against their oppressors.

One cannot say as much for the Rhinelanders, who were—whatever may be pretended to the contrary—not conscious of oppression but freely formed part of the German Empire, who remained loyal to Germany throughout the war: who, even now, proclaim their German nationality, and who, in spite of Dr. Dorten, are in large part opposed to any separation, and at the most favour a certain measure of independence. Further, the present movement, whose extent and strength can in the existing conditions hardly be ascertained, is obviously inspired by selfish motives. The Rhinelanders would desire to escape their share of the reparations burden. They would desire to escape the particularly painful consequences of another war which would fall upon them. The case of

Czecho-Slovakia and of Poland on the one hand and of Rhineland on the other are altogether different.

The French themselves, even the most Nationalist of Frenchmen, see plainly the arguments against supporting the Rhineland movement. They are perfectly aware of the motives which inspire Dr. Dorten. Why should the French, it is asked, take the responsibility for helping to constitute a new State whose gratitude towards them would be doubtful and whose loyalty could not be relied upon? Why should the French bear the cost of the creation of such a State? Why should they discredit themselves in the eyes of the world? They remember the protests against what was called "French imperialism" when the Separatists both in Rhineland and in the Palatinate employed the most dubious methods, the most disgraceful tactics, towards the end of 1923.

Why should the Rhinelanders escape the payment of reparations? Why should France lull herself into a sense of false security, for it is at least possible that when Germany seeks her revenge, the Rhinelanders, whether they have obtained their autonomy or not, will, as good Germans, march whole-heartedly with the rest of Germany against France.

General Gouraud, with whom I recently discussed this question, roundly declared that the strength of France lay in her unity. In spite of the variety of races, the mixed origins of France, which has been, owing to the geographical situation of the country, the melting-pot of Europe since the beginning of history, the French are undoubtedly a homogeneous nation. If there were in these modern days, when the consciousness of nationality has been sharpened, any kind of territorial acquisition, or rather a mere ambiguous racial extension, France would be divided and definitely weakened. The notion of a Rhineland Ally must be set completely aside. The notion even of the disintegration of the Reich is deceptive, as France may one day discover to her cost.

The Quai d'Orsay was impressed by these considerations, and in so far as the French were implicated in the Rhineland movement, it was without the authority or the consent of the Quai d'Orsay.

What becomes, then, of Dr. Dorten and his idea? Is he leading a forlorn hope? This does not necessarily follow. Much will depend upon the course of events. We have not yet done with the demand for some kind of autonomy, though precisely what form it will take it would be difficult to determine at the moment.

There is an answer to be found perhaps in the Treaty of Versailles. According to the Treaty, Rhineland is to be demilitarised for ever. But no machinery is provided for the demilitarisation of these regions. The French would be happy if some machinery could be devised, and it is not outside the bounds of possibility that the Germans also would be happy if a solution were to be found in the neutralisation of Rhineland. As for the Rhinelanders themselves, they would surely be content to evade military service, to be placed beyond the reach of militarism, whether French or German. They could wish for nothing better than the application of the Treaty in this respect. The bridge-heads of the Rhine, and the whole of the provinces on the left bank, should be exempt from military movements and military constructions. The chances of a war would thus be beyond question lessened. To provide the machinery for the effective application of these clauses of the Treaty, the French must be prepared to drive a bargain. They must be prepared to evacuate Rhineland before the expiration of the term laid down in the Treaty. In return for this evacuation, they might receive assurances which would be even more valuable to them than the pacts with the United States and with England, which were elaborated in 1919 but fell to the ground because they were not ratified. What assurances?

The proposal has been made, and it is the proposal which seems to offer the best chances of a peaceful solution of the protracted Franco-German quarrel, that the League of Nations should be asked to supervise the demilitarisation of Rhineland. The League of Nations should possess a small police force which would patrol the provinces, which would ascertain that no breach of the military clauses of the Treaty is committed, and which in the last resort, in the event of a fresh German aggression, would oppose a resistance which would doubtless be nominal, but would be sufficient, first, to make Germany hesitate; second, to hold up and delay any advance; and, third, to bring into the field against Germany the armies of all the countries whose flags have been flouted by Germany. For in the police force of the League of Nations there would be represented the flags of many nations belonging to the League, and although not directly engaged, the flags of all other nations who are members of the League would be flying somewhere in the background.

It is difficult to conceive a sensible country, even though animated by a spirit of revenge, disregarding the possibilities of antagonising the majority of the nations of the world. Here would be a genuine guarantee of peace. I confess that I know no other plan which is as satisfactory.

Dr. Dorten has not yet advocated precisely this solution. He stops short at the demand for a separate Rhineland Republic. He could not refuse such a solution were it to be put forward in the name of the nations represented in the League. I believe that sooner or later it will be put forward officially. Dr. Dorten has therefore perhaps builded better than he knew.

XX

Viscount Cecil—or, Lord Robert Cecil, as he was called before his promotion to the peerage when the title of Lord was merely given in courtesy—is undoubtedly the most active and distinguished European representative of the hope embodied in the League of Nations. As such, he deserves some study.

There are other protagonists of the League, who might have been taken. There is General Smuts, but his place is outside Europe, and in spite of occasional incursions into European affairs, he must be regarded rather as a local South African figure. Still, in those far-off days of the Paris Peace Conference, he did exceedingly useful work in helping to draft the somewhat unsatisfactory Covenant of the League.

There is, happily, still M. Léon Bourgeois, the real father of the League, with whom I constantly discussed the shape the organisation should take and who was good enough to regard me as one of his "collaborators." But M. Léon Bourgeois appears to have retired from public life, for the present, at least.

Lord Cecil remains almost alone among European statesmen, at once a pioneer and a participant in the affairs of the League. He advocates it unflinchingly in places where it is unpopular, and he has not spared himself in addressing public meetings, both in England and in France, in favour of the League. He does not regard it as a close corporation of government-appointed delegates, who can afford to be indifferent to public opinion. The League, he clearly sees, must be broad-based upon popular wishes or it is nothing. A mere diplomatic caucus sitting at Geneva is useless. There are plenty of diplomatic bodies—notably the Conference of Ambassadors—which can arrange quarrels quite as well as the League—unless the League in some special way represents the views of the people as well as of their rulers. I suspect that Lord Cecil would privately agree with this statement but would be reluctant to commit himself so far in public.

I remember a certain meeting at which something like a controversy sprang up upon this point. I contended—as I still contend—that the League would be capable of better work were it to detach itself entirely from the Foreign Offices and the State Departments. It would lose its official authority but it would be more truly expressive of the will of the peoples.

At present the Members of the League Council, which is the effective body, are nominated by their governments and represent their governments almost in the same sense as Ambassadors. They take their instructions almost as Ambassadors take instructions. Does it not follow that the Council must resemble the Conference of Ambassadors—that is to say, a purely governmental body which can accomplish nothing that does not suit the particular policies of the governments who are represented? The League Council can therefore in no way transcend ordinary diplomatic procedure. Perhaps it can give a little more dramatic background to such settlements that it effects.

Now, without going into details, which would take us outside the bounds of this sketch, surely it would be possible to devise a better method of representation which would assure the delegates complete independence! The reason why they have done so little with regard to disarmament, for example, which is, after all, the greatest task of the League, is that the Members of the Council have not put forward their own opinions, have not insisted on real solutions, have not, in a word, thought internationally but have thought nationally, as instructed to think by their governments. They have not felt that they were supported by public opinion but were merely the creatures of their governments.

We have had the clash of national antagonisms, and it is surprising in these circumstances that some of the Members and particularly Lord Cecil, have struck a deeper note. Almost the same thing is to be said of the League Assembly, which meets at least once a year. The Assembly is a larger body. It discusses whatever subjects arise with more freedom. It purports to draw its strength from public opinion rather than from the respective Governments. But nevertheless, even the Assembly has its Members appointed by the Governments, and once more one must express astonishment that it has spoken out on many occasions so strongly and has not left itself to be more fettered.

It should be observed in this connection that Lord Robert Cecil, as he then was, though undoubtedly the leading exponent of the League of Nations in England, was not nominated by the British Government as a British representative, but was obliged to enter the Assembly, as it were, by the back door. He would have been excluded, not because he did not sufficiently express the League idea but because he expressed it too well, had not General Smuts appointed him as the representative of South Africa.

This grotesque anomalous proceeding should have been sufficient to convince Lord Cecil that there is something wrong in the constitution of the League. It should have convinced him that a more popular form of representation is necessary if the League is to be saved from becoming not a true League of Nations, but a League of Foreign Offices.

One would rather that the League accomplished even less, provided it used the platform of Geneva to send out ringing messages to the world, at once to influence and to focus world opinion. The present system is rather calculated

to stifle the true promulgation of morality in
politics than to encourage it. The League as it
stands is frustrated. It is placed in leading-
strings by the governments; it is not, so to speak,
a conscience for the world. It is surely a conscience that is wanted!

One would have thought that this thesis would
have made a special appeal to Lord Cecil on
account of the personal treatment which he
received from the British Government, which
only desired, as did other European governments,
to make Members of the League men who would
adopt the narrow national diplomatic view.
But Lord Cecil is somewhat refractory to these
considerations because of his own Foreign Office
training. This, I think, is a pity, for his instincts
and his vision lead him beyond the necessarily
narrow views of the Foreign Offices. In the
meeting to which I have referred, he argued
against the radical reform of the constitution
of the League, which I have on several occasions
put forward. Others maintained that the League
could do nothing unless it were backed by the
governments and were an emanation of the
governments.

But what can it do if it is an emanation of the

governments that the governments themselves
could not have done without the League through
the existing machinery of diplomacy? What
most of us who helped in our humble way in the
formation of the League in 1919 had in mind
was an organisation which, while possessing no
absolute super-national powers, while unable to
impose its decisions on the governments, would
nevertheless draw its strength from a wider
moral sphere, and would gradually guide the
governments, which are obliged to think nationally, into international methods of thinking.

However this may be, and one recognises that
there is much to be said on either side, Lord
Cecil deserves the greatest praise because if he
nominally sticks tight to the Foreign Office conception, he has yet in practice soared above
that conception. His environment, both in his
early days and in his later days, was not such
as to induce the generosity of mind, the noble
aspirations which he has shown. He is the third
son of the third Marquis of Salisbury—the
famous Marquis of Salisbury who was Prime
Minister of England, who was exceedingly able
but who was a typical English Conservative.
The typical English Conservative cannot easily

treat foreign countries as being on quite the same footing as England. He seeks to make British interests prevail—a perfectly legitimate object, but not necessarily the object of a League of Nations.

Lord Robert, who is now sixty years of age, acted when a young man as secretary to his father. This was an admirable training but not the kind of training which might have been expected to make him a liberal-minded politician. His relations with the Marquis of Salisbury were not simply those of father and son, but of statesman and confidant. He was in the innermost secrets of the government; he knew the mainsprings of British policy.

Afterwards Lord Robert had a legal training. He was called to the Bar in 1887 and became a King's Counsel in 1900. Thus he learnt how to read and interpret documents, how to discover flaws in the reasoning of the other party. He learnt all the little *finesse* of discussion and the possibilities of persuasive eloquence. This knowledge has stood him in good stead. I have seen him save the situation at League Assemblies in Geneva and at Council meetings in Paris, by availing himself dexterously of a legal point. Legal points do not perhaps touch the merits of a case, but they often enable the expert practitioner to open the way for a compromise. They serve as a preliminary to a higher appeal. In this respect, Lord Robert was keen and skilful and assiduous.

Twice was Lord Robert actually at the Foreign Office, once in the early part of the war, when he was Parliamentary Under Secretary for Foreign Affairs, and again in 1918 when he was Assistant Secretary of State for Foreign Affairs. He came to Paris in 1919 to assist in the drafting of the constitution of the League of Nations. Afterwards, in a Conservative Government, he accepted the post of Lord Privy Seal. There are many English politicians who believe that he made a mistake in accepting this post, that he would have been better advised to have kept clear of party ties. There was a moment when his name was in men's mouths as a possible Prime Minister of some new or renovated party formed on liberal lines.

But whether his parliamentary career as a commoner may be regarded as a success or a failure—he was never sufficiently the party man to attain complete parliamentary success—he will be remembered as the sincere and indefatigable worker for the League of Nations, not only in England but on the Continent, where his name is among the best known of European statesmen. He has now gone to the House of Lords, where perhaps his political possibilities of action are further limited, but he is more than ever ardent in the cause of the League.

His personal appearance is familiar to readers of newspapers all over the world because he is one of those fortunate individuals who lend themselves readily to the pencil of the caricaturist. He is thin, with stooping shoulders and a hawklike face held well forward. He is the perfect form of a living question mark. But if his parliamentary career gave rise to considerable speculation, he was never in himself an enigma. He is straightforward and earnest, and once he had found the cause for which he could wholeheartedly work, he threw himself into his particular predestined job with remarkable zeal.

The League of Nations, even though Germany, Russia, and, above all, the United States, are absent, so that it becomes half a League, is half a league onward. Despite its demi-successes and its semi-failures, it is and will be the world's

greatest guarantee against war. Last year it
was menaced in its very existence. This nation
and that nation threatened to withdraw when
the trouble arose over Corfu. If once the
process of dislocation begins, secession will
rapidly follow secession. Happily the danger
has passed.

The European governments are now inclined
to trust the League. Europe's most enlightened
thinkers consider it to be imperative for Europe
that the League be saved. It must grow in
strength as the years go on. For, if it disappears,
there is a frank reversion to the idea of force
in the settlement of international quarrels.
However imperfectly, it stands for justice and
peace. Its break-up would be regarded with
dismay. Pessimism would indeed be justified.
One would feel that, conditions being as they
are, its absence would infallibly mean injustice
and war.

It cannot yet tackle the great problems; but
its record of work of a secondary kind is, with
all the drawbacks which I have indicated, at
least encouraging, and the governments themselves realise that unless they accord more confidence to the League, they will find themselves

unable to restore a continent, which has been devastated from end to end during the past ten years. The seeds of disruption are everywhere. As quickly as one evil is rooted up another evil springs like a weed apace. It would be well not to give way to the natural disappointment that is felt by most of those who supported the conception and organisation of the League in its early stages. Hopes were raised high, perhaps far too high. Europe, and to some extent, America, dreamt of a better order of things which would be instituted immediately after the war. There was to have been a new heaven and a new earth. The League was to have been the regenerating miracle of our time.

It is impossible not to contrast the performances of the League, and above all, its general exhibition of weakness, of a desire for compromise on essentially basic ideas, with the bright beliefs of those days when it was, doubtless foolishly, thought that automatically, disputes between nations would be quietly referred to the League and as quietly settled to everybody's satisfaction.

That is the tragedy of human aspirations.

One exaggerates the immediate possibilities with the result that in face of realities one is plunged in despair.

"As high as we have mounted in delight,
  In our dejection do we sink as low."

The League was to have done everything instantly. It is now pretended that the League can do nothing for ever. But these alternations of feeling are foolish. The truth about the League lies somewhere between the exaggerated expectations and the broken promises.

There is neither complete fulfilment nor total frustration. There can be no sudden and radical change in the conduct of the world's affairs, but when the League was begun, a new factor came into diplomacy, and it is a factor that will become more powerful with time. An effective League must necessarily be a plant of slow growth. It will have to be nursed along to perfection. The League will have to learn by experience and practice. It will be more and more trusted because there is in the last resort no middle course between unrestrained nationalism and mutual destruction on the one hand,

and on the other hand, internationalism and mutual co-operation.

The main need of the League is time. I have heard Lord Cecil make out a fairly good case for the actual achievements of the League. He is an enthusiast and he is an able advocate. But it would be equally possible to argue that the League has on many occasions, and indeed, mostly, failed hitherto. Without the League it is to be doubted whether Austria would have been restored to decent conditions of existence. But the partition of Upper Silesia by the League was probably a bad piece of business which will produce the most unpleasant consequences.

The League has prevented minor disputes from developing on dangerous lines. That is to its credit. But the League refrained from dealing faithfully with the problem of the Ruhr, a hole out of which the wealth of Europe ran fast, and which the League did not even attempt to caulk.

The League was useful where little nations were concerned, but when challenged by a great power, such as Italy, in the affair of Corfu, the League was afraid to act. But argument both for and against the League is futile. It is too early to draw up the balance of bad and good. It is in its embryonic stage. It must be developed. It would be absurd to judge a man by his infant days. Achievement is not, as we sometimes stupidly suppose, the first thing but the last thing. Much has to lead up to achievement.

We have to ask what the League may do, what it will undoubtedly do in the future, if it is kept in being. We have not to ask what it has done in a past of four or five years. The child must first grow up. It has to contend with many handicaps. It was repudiated, be it remembered, by one of its creators. It was deprived of assistance which it had a right to expect.

Whether the League is doing well or not, is somewhat irrelevant. The League needs time and while it has such fine workers in its behalf as Lord Cecil, and the pick of Europe's best citizens, men and women, it cannot fail to increase in strength, until one day it will fulfil its promise and the world will become conscious of its interdependence and its solidarity.